JEAN STAFFORD

A Study of the Short Fiction

Twayne's Studies in Short Fiction

Gordon Weaver, General Editor
Oklahoma State University

JEAN STAFFORD
*Photograph courtesy of Stafford Collection, Special Collections Department,
University of Colorado at Boulder Libraries.*

JEAN STAFFORD

A Study of the Short Fiction

Mary Ann Wilson
University of Southwestern Louisiana

TWAYNE PUBLISHERS
An Imprint of Simon & Schuster Macmillan
New York

Prentice Hall International
London   Mexico City   New Delhi   Singapore   Sydney   Toronto

Twayne's Studies in Short Fiction Series, No. 62

Copyright © 1996 by Twayne Publishers

Twayne Publishers
An Imprint of Simon & Schuster Macmillan
866 Third Avenue
New York, New York 10022

Library of Congress Cataloging-in-Publication Data

Wilson, Mary Ann.
   Jean Stafford : a study of the short fiction / Mary Ann Wilson.
     p.   cm. — (Twayne's studies in short fiction ; no. 62)
   Includes bibliographical references and index.
   ISBN 0-8057-7807-1 (cloth)
    1. Stafford, Jean, 1915–   —Criticism and interpretation.
   2. Women and literature—United States—History—20th century.
   3. Short story.   I. Title.   II. Series.
   PS3569.T2Z93   1995
   813'.54—dc20   95-23493
                                                   CIP

10 9 8 7 6 5 4 3 2 1

Printed in the United States of America

To my husband and colleague, Jim

Contents

Contents

Preface

Writing is a private, an almost secret enterprise carried on within the heart and mind in a room whose doors are closed; the shock is staggering when the doors are flung open and the eyes of strangers are trained on the naked and the newborn.

—Jean Stafford, "An Etiquette for Writers"

Technique, we know, is seldom void of moral implications; it is often a strategy of the imagination against despair.

—Ihab Hassan, *Radical Innocence: Studies in the Contemporary American Novel*

Jean Stafford (1915–79) wrote three novels and more than 40 short stories that collectively merit her a place among the finest fiction writers of her generation. The recent reissue of her Pulitzer Prize–winning *Collected Stories* and her 1947 novel *The Mountain Lion*, the appearance of three biographies in the last seven years, and the frequent anthologizing of her short stories attest to a renewed interest in and appreciation of this "writer's writer" whose first and only passion was her craft.

As yet there has been no in-depth study of Jean Stafford's short fiction—the genre she perfected and the one most critics agree represents her major achievement. These short stories appeared in prestigious literary journals such as the *Kenyon Review* and the *Partisan Review* and most frequently in the *New Yorker*, whose fiction editor Katharine White served as both personal and professional resource for Stafford as her career developed. They have been praised by contemporary writers of short fiction such as Joyce Carol Oates, who sees in Stafford a kindred spirit both immersed in the realistic details of her fictional worlds and ironically detached from them.

The enduring subject of Stafford's short fiction is the lives of girls and women from childhood to old age and the fears and anxieties they suffer at every stage. (Stafford wrote only nine stories with boys or men as central characters, and she included only two of these in her *Collected Stories*.) Although Stafford derided the ideologies of the women's movement in the 1960s and 1970s in her later years, in her fiction she treated issues of female self-definition, powerlessness, and marginality with remarkable sensitivity. Though she continued to resist the label "woman writer" and objected to any identification of her work as part of a female literary tradition, in her own life and art she continually examined issues central to the female subject in modern and contemporary settings. In a sense, Stafford kept rewriting her own life in these stories as she tried to reconcile the conflicts in her past through her fiction. In her recent biography of Jean Stafford, *The Interior Castle*, Ann Hulbert distinguishes between writing autobiographically "in the most direct, concrete sense" and "writing autobiographically in a thematic sense";[1] Stafford usually did the latter, since in her best stories the naked autobiographical facts were filtered through the ironic lens of emotional and psychological distance.

Born in Covina, California, but living her childhood and adolescence in the rugged landscape of Colorado, Jean escaped as soon as she could—first to Heidelberg to study philology and thereafter to Boston, New York, London, and Paris as she tried to separate herself geographically from what she viewed as her provincial western roots. But the roots went deeper than she knew, as she admits in the preface to her *Collected Stories*, and she continued to return to the West of her childhood in a series of brilliant short stories, some of which appear in the section titled "Cowboys and Indians, and Magic Mountains" from her 1969 *Collected Stories*. Growing up female in the rugged West is also the subject of perhaps her best novel, *The Mountain Lion*.

The cultural defensiveness Stafford felt about growing up out West was complicated by her father's failed ambitions as a writer of westerns. Significantly, she invokes his memory in the preface to *Collected Stories* when she refers to his pen names, Jack Wonder and Ben Delight, and his one published work, *When Cattle Kingdom Fell*. John Stafford grew increasingly bitter as his long, rambling works were rejected by publishers, finally refusing to work to support his family. Stafford's mother took in boarders to pay the bills, much to Jean's embarrassment. This complex family dynamic haunted Jean in her choice of a writing career and the almost perverse attraction she felt toward the domestic. Associating her father with the intellectual in her nature and her mother with the domestic, Jean would vacillate between the two throughout her life, often retreating into domesticity to avoid writing. The troubled childhood resulting from these early parental conflicts surfaces in some of her best short stories: "Bad Characters," "The Healthiest Girl in

Town," and "The Bleeding Heart." Father figures are largely absent from her work.

As she attempted to escape her Colorado past, Jean Stafford adopted other regions—Europe, Boston, Manhattan—peopling them with grown-up versions of the lonely, alienated children she treats so compassionately. Always imbued with a strong sense of place like her avowed literary mentors Henry James and Mark Twain, Stafford sought in geography what she lost in time—stability, order, and harmony. The genteel eastern ways and European sophistication she yearned for in early adolescence find their way into her stories of Boston and New England and the adventures of her alienated innocents abroad in Europe. Permeating these stories is the irony of Stafford's mature vision, always questioning and judging the dreams of her characters, who are all rootless—"displaced," to use her own term—never at home either geographically or spiritually. Time and again in her stories, illusion clashes with harsh reality, and in their Joycean exile her characters exchange one place for another but keep their acute loneliness—from the feisty Emily Vanderpool of "Bad Characters" to the poignant, aging beauty Angelica Early in "The End of a Career."

But irony in Stafford is no mere literary technique. Instead, as Josephine Hendin notes in her study of post-1945 fiction, *Vulnerable People*, irony is "an angle of vision from which we view ourselves. More than any other device, irony bridges the distance between our sense of vulnerability and our dreams of power."[2] Irony became the defensive posture Jean Stafford adopted in her fiction and in her life.

The landscape of Stafford's short fiction is littered with missed connections, unsaid words, and disillusioned lovers, all of which form a thematic pattern of loss and alienation, but Stafford's implicit belief in the shaping power of language and in the craft of the short story form mitigates what would otherwise be an unremittingly bleak vision. Growing up in the shadow of the great male moderns, Joyce and Eliot, and reaching artistic maturity in a New Critical milieu gave Stafford a view of the artistic life and the exacting devotion it required. Though she struggled with the stern demands of her chosen profession, she never lost sight of its value.

As secretary to the *Southern Review* in 1940–41 and wife of the poet Robert Lowell, Stafford was immersed in a literary life at a crucial time in her career. She watched literary reputations being made in the cramped quarters of the *Review* and suffered through late night, drunken poetry readings by Lowell and his circle of fellow poets John

Berryman, Delmore Schwartz, and Randall Jarrell (memorialized in her masterful short story "An Influx of Poets"). Forced to retype drafts of Lowell's poems if he changed so much as a comma, Jean saw the painstaking evolution of a literary text and internalized from these experiences a belief in the power of the carefully chosen word. Always a meticulous reviser, Stafford reworked her short stories again and again, and with the help of editors like Katharine White, created a body of short fiction a new generation is beginning to discover. Though she never resolved in fiction the conflicts of her own troubled life, like her contemporaries Mary McCarthy and Katherine Anne Porter, Jean Stafford demythologized the female experience and thereby articulated the pressure points of an alienated postwar generation. The form most conducive to Stafford's unique voice was the short story, in whose brief, epiphanic moments she captured haunting fragments of experience that still resonate in our postmodern age.

Following Stafford's example in her *Collected Stories*, I divide my study of her short fiction in part 1 by her own regional headings: The Innocents Abroad; The Bostonians and Other Manifestations of the American Scene; Cowboys and Indians, and Magic Mountains; Manhattan Island. I am aware that Stafford felt such a grouping arbitrary, for whether her characters inhabit the rugged, mountainous West, the pseudogenteel East, or a European landscape, their world is blighted and their anomie a function not of place but of the human condition. Nevertheless, the palpable setting of these stories often emerges as strongly as character, making us aware of Jean Stafford's acute sense of place.

Within each of these regional headings I examine a representative sample of major and minor stories from her collections—*Children Are Bored on Sunday* (1953), *Bad Characters* (1964), *Selected Stories* (1966), and *The Collected Stories* (1969)—as well as the best of her uncollected works, including her last two stories, excerpted by her editor Robert Giroux from her unfinished novel *The Parliament of Women*: "An Influx of Poets" (1978) and "Woden's Day" (1979). My discussions of the stories cover the circumstances of composition and give a detailed reading, noting themes, techniques, and relation to her novels and essays where relevant. My readings of some of the stories incorporate summaries of Katharine White's editorial commentary, which often helped shape the final version of Stafford's work.

Part 2 contains Jean Stafford's own critical comments about writing fiction. Though Stafford made few critical pronouncements and seemed to find the magisterial pose of critic somewhat intimidating, the few statements she did make about her work are revealing. Perhaps because of her obsession with her own personal history, she frequently cautioned against a too close adherence to the material of one's life and preached instead an ironic detachment that became her most potent fictional weapon.

Part 3 presents a sampling of critical essays on Stafford placing her in various contexts—from the alienated postwar generation to a female literary tradition. I attempt in this section to give some idea of the range of critical approaches to Stafford's short fiction, from the earliest responses to the present. This section concludes with two personal reminiscences by friends of Jean Stafford.

The bibliography includes carefully selected entries chosen to give the new researcher as well as the more experienced a historical overview of the major works dealing with Stafford and her literary generation. Wanda Avila's 1983 bibliography of Jean Stafford, published by Garland Press, was an invaluable source in preparing this book.

I wish to thank the University of Southwestern Louisiana for a faculty research grant that enabled me to visit the Jean Stafford Collection at the University of Colorado to look at previously unpublished material. I am especially grateful to Kris McCusker and the staff in Special Collections, University of Colorado at Boulder, for their untiring help locating manuscripts, transcribing letters to and from Stafford, and supporting my project.

Notes

1. Ann Hulbert, *The Interior Castle: The Art and Life of Jean Stafford* (New York: Alfred A. Knopf, 1992), 278; hereafter cited in the text.
2. Josephine Hendin, *Vulnerable People: A View of American Fiction since 1945* (Oxford: Oxford University Press, 1978), 11.

Acknowledgments

The author gratefully acknowledges permission to quote from the following:

Excerpts from the following stories by Jean Stafford, cited by permission of Russell & Volkening, Inc., as agents for the author: "The Home Front," "The Maiden," "The Echo and the Nemesis," *A Winter's Tale*, "My Blithe, Sad Bird," "The Children's Game," "Maggie Meriwether's Rich Experience," "Caveat Emptor," "Polite Conversation," "A Country Love Story," "An Influx of Poets," "The Interior Castle," "The Bleeding Heart," "Life Is No Abyss," "And Lots of Solid Color," "The Darkening Moon," "The Healthiest Girl in Town," "The Violet Rock," "Bad Characters," "A Reading Problem," "The Scarlet Letter," "The Liberation," "The Mountain Day," "The Tea Time of Stouthearted Ladies," "The Philosophy Lesson," "In the Zoo," "A Summer Day," "A Reasonable Facsimile," "Woden's Day," "Cops and Robbers," "Between the Porch and the Altar," "Children Are Bored on Sunday," "The Captain's Gift," "I Love Someone," "Beatrice Trueblood's Story," and "The End of a Career."

Excerpts from Jean Stafford's "An Etiquette for Writers," reprinted by permission of the Jean Stafford Collection, Special Collections Department, University of Colorado at Boulder Libraries, and by permission of Russell & Volkening, Inc., as agents for the author. © 1952 by Jean Stafford. Excerpts from Jean Stafford's "Truth in Fiction," reprinted from *Library Journal* 91 (1966): 4557–4565. Stafford, Jean. Copyright © 1966 by Reed Publishing, USA. Excerpts from Jean Stafford's "The Felicities of Formal Education," reprinted by permission of the Jean Stafford Collection, Special Collections Department, University of Colorado at Boulder Libraries, and by permission of Russell & Volkening, Inc., as agents for the author. Copyright © 1971 by Jean Stafford. Excerpts from Jean Stafford's "Men, Women, Language, Science, and Other Dichotomies," first published in *Confrontation* 7 (1973): 69–74, Long Island University. Reprinted by permission. Excerpts from Jean Stafford's "Miss McKeehan's Pocketbook," published in *Colorado Quarterly* 24 (1976): 407–11. Reprinted by permission of the University of Colorado, Boulder, Colorado.

Excerpts from Ihab Hassan's "Jean Stafford: The Expense of Style and the Scope of Sensibility," *Western Review* 19 (1955): 185–203. Reprinted by permission of the author. © by Ihab Hassan. Excerpts from Olga W. Vickery's "Jean Stafford and the Ironic Vision," *South Atlantic Quarterly* 61:4. Copyright Duke University Press, 1962. Reprinted with permission. Excerpts from Chester Eisinger's *Fiction of the Forties* (Chicago: University of Chicago Press, 1963), 231–33, 294–307. © 1963 by Chester E. Eisinger. Excerpts from Jerome Mazzaro's "Remembrances of Things Proust," *Shenandoah* 16 (1965): 114–17. Reprinted from *Shenandoah*: The Washington and Lee University Review, with the permission of the Editor. Excerpts from Guy Davenport's "Tough Characters, Solid Novels," *National Review*, 26 January 1965, 66. © 1965 by *National Review*, Inc. Reprinted by permission. Excerpts from Mary Hegel Wagner's review of *The Collected Stories of Jean Stafford*, *America*, April 1969, 426–27. Reprinted by permission of *America* magazine. Excerpts from Sid Jenson's "The Noble Wicked West of Jean Stafford," *Western American Literature* 7 (1973): 261–70. Reprinted by permission. Excerpts from Melody Graulich's "Jean Stafford's Western Childhood: Huck Finn Joins the Camp Fire Girls," *Denver Quarterly*, Vol. 18, No. 1 (1983): 39–55. Reprinted by permission. Text of Joyce Carol Oates's "The Interior Castle: The Art of Jean Stafford's Short Fiction," *Shenandoah* 30 (1979): 61–64. Reprinted from *Shenandoah*: The Washington and Lee University Review, with the permission of the Editor. Excerpts from Philip Stevick's *Alternative Pleasures: Postrealist Fiction and the Tradition* (Urbana: University Press of Illinois, 1981). © 1981 by the Board of Trustees of the University of Illinois. Excerpts from Maureen Ryan's *Innocence and Estrangement in the Fiction of Jean Stafford*. Copyright © 1987 by Louisiana State University Press. Used with permission. Excerpts from Bruce Bawer's "Jean Stafford's Triumph," *New Criterion* 7 (1988): 61–72. Reprinted by permission of the author. Excerpts from Dorothea Straus's "Jean Stafford," *Shenandoah* 30 (1979): 85–91. Reprinted from *Shenandoah*: The Washington and Lee University Review, with the permission of the Editor. Excerpts from Peter Taylor's "A Commemorative Tribute to Jean Stafford," *Shenandoah* 30 (1979): 56–60. Reprinted from *Shenandoah*: The Washington and Lee University Review, with the permission of the Editor.

Part 1

THE SHORT FICTION

Introduction

Jean Stafford and the New Criticism

Jean Stafford's marriage to Robert Lowell in 1940 and her subsequent move to Baton Rouge to become secretary of the *Southern Review* plunged her into an intensely literary environment—a rigid, formalist world, hierarchical and determined largely by successful male writers. As documented in my article "In Another Country: Jean Stafford's Literary Apprenticeship in Baton Rouge,"[1] at this formative time in her career Jean had constant access to incoming manuscripts in the *Review* office, read the incisive critical comments on these manuscripts by editors Cleanth Brooks and Robert Penn Warren, and experienced on a personal level the tensions and ironies of a literary vocation. Like her early mentor James Joyce—and his literary descendants the New Critics—Stafford came to believe in the value and necessity of form as a way of harnessing inchoate experience. Stafford criticism consistently notes that she imposes on her fiction an order and structure—a timelessness—gratefully at odds with her shifting fortunes.

Her own troubled life perhaps strengthened her belief in another major tenet of New Criticism, the impersonality of the writer. Having been cautioned by Ford Madox Ford about the dangers of writing too close to life, Stafford would struggle with this autobiographical impulse throughout her life, writing several novels in manuscript dealing with painful events from her college years, such as the suicide of Lucy Cooke, a close friend, and working intermittently throughout her life on an autobiographical novel, *The Parliament of Women*, which she never finished. Her last two published stories are excerpted from this unfinished text. Clearly, her best stories evidence an ironic detachment from the merely personal and contain instead a healthy dose of the aesthetic distance the New Critics counseled. Thus, while Brooks and Warren and their disciples were revolutionizing the teaching of literature in the universities, Stafford was reading proof on *Southern Review* articles espousing similarly antihistoricist tenets and having conflicted thoughts about the meaning—indeed, the possibility—of her own literary vocation. As she cryptically notes in her 1966 essay "Truth in Fiction," "[W]rite for yourself and God and a few close friends, and if you meet the exacting demands of this group . . . you can devote your whole attention to the really important agony of getting through a writing day."[2] In retrospect, Stafford absorbed the critical imperatives of irony, paradox, and tension; the integrity of a story or poem; and the disciplined rigor of the artistic life as she struggled to meet the demands of an exacting job and an exacting marriage.

Jean Stafford and the *New Yorker*

It is perhaps fitting that the magazine the young Jean Stafford wrote so earnestly about in her journals as the epitome of eastern sophistication should, by 1978, have published 22 of her short stories. Harold Ross, its founder and editor, had grown up in Colorado like Stafford, and as Charlotte Goodman notes in her biography of Stafford, he was sympathetic to new, unestablished writers.[3] From its inception the *New Yorker* had also been more receptive to women writers than the quarterlies, and with the acquisition of Katharine White as fiction editor, the stage was set for writers like Jean Stafford to appear in its pages.

With a cultured New England background and impeccable credentials from Bryn Mawr, Katharine Angell (later married to E. B. White, another *New Yorker* contributor) was hired by Harold Ross as a part-time reader of manuscripts in 1925, shortly after the *New Yorker*'s debut. She quickly moved up to editor and, as Scott Elledge notes in his biography of E. B. White, persuaded Harold Ross that the magazine should publish "short stories that were just as distinctive, original, and contemporary as its cartoons."[4] Indeed, she was largely responsible for promoting and encouraging what has since become known as the typical *New Yorker* story: one that de-emphasizes plot and focuses instead on nuances of character and situation. The fact that some of Jean Stafford's stories of this period fit White's model perhaps accounts for the young editor's enthusiastic response to Stafford's submissions. But the range and variety of writers and stories appearing in the magazine, as well as the variety of Stafford's *New Yorker* pieces, belie such a formulaic label. As Stafford would attest years later in a 1971 lecture to Barnard College students, there is no such thing as a *New Yorker* story. She went on to enumerate such diverse writers as John Cheever, J. D. Salinger, Isaac Singer, William Faulkner, and Flannery O'Connor—maintaining that such distinctive voices make it ridiculous to speak of a generic *New Yorker* story.[5] Stafford's stories appearing in the *New Yorker* do, in fact, range widely: from the rugged western setting and first-person, colloquial narration of "Bad Characters" (1954) to the European decadence and urbane tone of "My Blithe, Sad Bird" (1957).

From the appearance of her first *New Yorker* story, "Children Are Bored on Sunday" (1948), to her last, "An Influx of Poets" (1978), Stafford and Katharine White sustained a mutually beneficial personal and professional relationship, documented in a 30-year correspondence. Initially drawn together in 1947 at stressful times in their lives—Stafford emerging from a sanitarium in New York after her divorce from Robert Lowell, and White recovering from a painful spinal operation—the two women, according to White's biographer Linda Davis, were to share a lifetime of physical ailments, personal tragedies, and artistic triumphs.[6] (White even arranged a meeting in London between Stafford and her third husband, A. J. Liebling.) White's aristocratic bearing and Ivy League education appealed to the young Stafford, 22 years White's junior; Stafford's physical and emotional suffering brought out the older woman's maternal solicitude. They shared a keen intelligence and meticulous eye for detail, resulting in Stafford's willingness to follow White's editorial suggestions, though admittedly her polished manuscripts required little grammatical or syntactic editing. White's comments on Stafford's short stories are more contextual, noting flaws in character motivation or plot inconsistencies. The final product of such fruitful collaboration was inevitably a tighter, more focused story. At one point in Stafford's career when she was suffering from writer's block, Katharine White even gave her an idea for a story, based on an incident White had heard about. The resulting story, "The Mountain Day," appeared in the magazine in 1956.

What seems clear, looking back on Jean Stafford's life, is that Katharine White (and to a lesser extent other women writers such as Evelyn Scott) served as a female literary community for Stafford, reminiscent of Lowell and his generation of doomed poets, or Cleanth Brooks and Robert Penn Warren and their fledgling critical movement during the Louisiana State University period. Perpetually insecure about her provincial childhood and frightened of the New York literati whose withering cocktail party banter she had witnessed firsthand, Stafford craved approval and desperately needed encouragement from a woman like Katharine White, who represented the eastern literary establishment but who genuinely admired Stafford and gave her work a sympathetic reading. White had a marvelous gift for making each writer she edited feel unique and valued, and this kind of support gave Jean Stafford the objective critical judgment she needed as an artist, as well as the surrogate mothering this self-styled "orphan" frequently invited.[7] As William Leary aptly notes, if and when contemporary readers remember Jean Stafford, it is rarely for her novels. Instead, they remember her *New Yorker* stories, a fact that would no doubt please Katharine White, to whom Stafford dedicated her *Collected Stories*.[8]

Jean Stafford and a Female Literary Tradition

Jean Stafford came of age among a generation of literary women for whom the study of gender construction was not as central as it has since become and to whom the idea of a female literary tradition was only beginning to make itself heard. Certainly, Mary McCarthy's *Memories of a Catholic Girlhood* and Carson McCullers's *Ballad of the Sad Café* or *Member of the Wedding*, as well as Jean Stafford's *Boston Adventure* and *The Mountain Lion*, all anticipate later feminist issues of female self-definition, powerlessness, and socially constructed gender roles, but for the most part female contemporaries of Jean Stafford were writing out of a male modernist tradition—and in the case of writers such as Stafford, Caroline Gordon, and Mary McCarthy, were literally married to central figures in the tradition. Stafford, in her later years, would in fact rail against aspects of the incipient women's movement, focusing on insignificant details such as the use of "Ms." or genderless nouns and pronouns,[9] or writing a scathing review of Simone de Beauvoir's *Les Belles Images* (1968), maintaining that it was precisely the kind of work to elicit the pejorative label "woman writer" from male critics.[10] Further, she pointedly allies herself to male literary models, Mark Twain and Henry James, rarely acknowledging any debt to other women writers.

Yet as Ann Hulbert's recent biography of Stafford points out, though she rejected the label "woman writer" and "anything that might be described as a feminine literary tradition," Stafford was constantly and painfully aware of "the pressures that male influence and expectation exerted on her" (Hulbert, xiii). Like her contemporary and sometime mentor, Caroline Gordon, Stafford paradoxically both devalued her work and resisted the essentializing label of "woman writer," often deflecting her own confusion about her chosen vocation onto easy targets like the women's movement. Perhaps it is fair to speculate that the literary audience Stafford envisioned for her works was thus emphatically male, though satisfying even this exacting male audience was not enough, as Jean's 1947 letter to Robert Lowell indicates. After hearing Randall Jarrell's praise for her second novel, *The Mountain Lion*, Stafford wrote to Lowell, "Why should it console me to be praised as a good writer? . . . [T]here is no thing worse for a woman than to be deprived of her womanliness. For me, there is nothing worse than the knowledge that life holds nothing for me but being a writer."[11] Such painfully self-effacing statements reveal a profound ambivalence about her literary vocation on both the personal and the professional levels. If topics concerning women emerge from Stafford's fiction—and they do—they were always secondary in her mind to both the human dilemma the works dramatize and the aesthetic problems such as character consistency a particular story poses.

Limited by their creator's own historical shortsightedness, Stafford's women rarely triumph. Instead, they compromise, fall prey to illusion, or resign themselves to a life of loneliness and alienation: Angelica Early in "The End of a Career" sees growing old as the end of her life as a beauty; Beatrice Trueblood in "Beatrice Trueblood's Story" capitulates to a loveless marriage; even the young Sue Ledbetter in "The Echo and the Nemesis," though she escapes physically from her, is haunted by the memory of her grotesquely fat, demented roommate. Sonie Marburg in *Boston Adventure* laments the fact that she is a woman, yearning for the intellectual freedom her friend Nathan seems to possess. Perhaps more to the point, Stafford kills off her intellectually precocious young Molly in *The Mountain Lion*, unable to envision a future for the budding writer. Permeating all of Stafford's works is the lingering question of identity or self-authentication in a largely inhospitable, unloving world. That the forms this self-authentication takes are invariably grounded in the female experience demonstrates Jean Stafford's concern with issues contemporary feminist theory has yet to resolve. As Maureen Ryan aptly notes, Stafford uses woman as a vehicle or symbol for the universal angst she dramatizes.[12]

The Innocents Abroad

Because Jean Stafford consciously appropriated titles from other writers, her choice of Mark Twain's 1869 work, *Innocents Abroad*, as the title for one of the sections of her *Collected Stories* evokes several levels of literary influence. Readers familiar with Twain's work will remember its subtitle as *The New Pilgrim's Progress*, a fact that illuminates what recent Stafford critics have noted as the quest-romance form in her work.[13] Stafford's characters not only embody the restlessness and dislocation critics of American literature have isolated as central to the American character, but they also dramatize the archetypal conflict between innocence and experience such writers as Mark Twain and Henry James found so intriguing. Just as Mark Twain explores the realities behind the myths of Old and New Worlds, Stafford similarly rejects any reductive equation of the male quest with expansiveness and the female with circumscription. Her innocents abroad, whether male or female, share a radical alienation and a fragile sense of self that are often reflected in the historical upheavals framing their personal lives. Though Jean Stafford's primary focus in her short stories was on the marginalized lives of girls and women, her male characters often confront the same cruel limitations, as the earliest of the stories in this grouping demonstrates.

"The Home Front," appearing in the *Partisan Review* in 1945, explores both regional and cultural innocence through the figure of Dr. Alfred Pakheiser, a German Jew living in an American lodging house during World War II.[14] Charlotte Goodman observes that the bleak Connecticut setting of this story reflects the town of Black Rock, Connecticut, where Stafford and Lowell lived after his release from prison for draft evasion (139). In any case, the theme of exile introduced here anticipates many of Stafford's later works. Firmly grounded in a historical period, the story has an ironic title that captures the impermanence of wartime and frames the cultural hatred and mistrust Stafford expresses through Dr. Pakheiser and his anti-Semitic Hungarian landlady, Mrs. Horvath. Nostalgic for the Heidelberg of his youth, Pakheiser realizes wryly that, just as in those days, his only friend is the gray tomcat who visits him daily. The palpable hatred of Dr. Pakheiser and Mrs. Horvath mirrors the larger war in the background; Mrs. Horvath's son's hobby of catching birds is as unnatural as the wartime act of taking prisoners. Implicitly, Stafford suggests that irrational prejudices—whether against cats, birds, or Jews—destroy the fabric of humanity and doom us to misunderstandings both large and small.

Like Twain's pilgrims, Pakheiser is a victim of the illusory world that exists only in his mind: the "imagined" America the *Quaker City* travelers invariably compare to the barbaric realities of Europe or the Near East. He romanticizes his student days in Heidelberg; ignores the industrial dump behind his rooming house, preferring to gaze through the other windows overlooking the water and imagine himself in the country; and individualizes his grim boardinghouse room with pictures and objects from his past, pretending his temporary "home front" is indeed home. But the doctor's greatest illusion is that, unlike the Horvaths, he harbors no prejudice. With unrelenting irony Stafford allows us to see the world according to Pakheiser: he refers to the Horvaths as "savages," imagines them eating gross foods and fat meat, wonders if they ever bathe or brush their teeth, and, with chilling clarity, observes Mrs. Horvath's "flat Magyar nose" (*CABS*, 118). Adding to the doctor's painful isolation are his almost female refinement and sensitivity, his worry that he is becoming "an old lady," and his fear of Mrs. Horvath's veiled accusations of his unmanliness. Victims of the same prejudices about each other, these "allies" wage war on all fronts: countries, nationalities, genders. The story's carefully plotted, four-part structure ironically undercuts its depiction of the randomness of human violence and the mindless hatred underlying all prejudice.

Another Heidelberg story with a male protagonist is Stafford's 1950 *New Yorker* piece "The Maiden."[15] Its disaffected main character is an American journalist, Evan Leckie, whose wife has just left him and who, recently "transferred to Heidelberg from the squalor and perdition of Nuremberg" (*CS*, 55), is feeling disoriented and rootless. The story's compressed setting is a post–World War II dinner party in Heidelberg of Germans and Americans, a sophisticated, eclectic group whose conversation inevitably turns to the ravages of war and a nostalgia for Germany's opulent past. Evan is entranced by the charming German couple, the Reinmuths, particularly the gentle, wifely Frau Reinmuth, whose seeming detachment from the horrors and indignities of war evokes a timeless and seductive world. In her unabashed love of the past and its artifacts such as the crystal wine decanters of their hostess, in her intensely feminine demeanor, but especially in her equally obvious and intense love for her husband, Frau Reinmuth seems the antithesis of Evan's resolutely modern wife, who dates everything from the year of her birth, 1920. As the evening progresses, this ethereal German couple comes to symbolize to the itinerant American journalist everything of value disappearing from the world: "And Evan Leckie, to whom the genesis of war had always been incomprehensible, looked with astonishment at these two pacific Germans and pondered how the whole hideous mistake had come about, what Eumenides had driven this pair to hardship, humiliation, and exile. Whatever else they were, however alien their values might be, these enemies were, *sub specie aeternitatis*, of incalculable worth if for no other reason than that, in an unloving world, they loved" (*CS*, 61).

But Judge Reinmuth shatters the ephemeral unity of this social gathering when he tells the story of his first case, a seemingly innocuous dinner party anecdote that ends on a grimly ironic note. As a young lawyer in Nuremberg, the Judge unsuccessfully defended a young man who confessed to stealing a paltry amount from an old woman. Invited by engraved invitation to the young man's guillotining, Reinmuth and his cohorts in formal dress watch the deceptively civilized spectacle of executioners in spotless white gloves silhouetted against a beautiful May morning. Rather than being repulsed at the violent ritual, Reinmuth confesses to an illogical euphoria that inspired him to call his young girlfriend on the telephone and propose. When he finishes his lugubrious tale, the Frau gazes lovingly at her husband of 20 years, remembering the romance of their long-ago courtship.

As a pall settles over the assembled dinner guests, they stare at each other, uncomprehendingly, over an immense cultural divide— the Americans shocked and repelled by the brutality concealed under a thin layer of civilization, the Germans apparently oblivious of anything contradictory in their behavior. Native American innocence might have led Evan to conclude that, in this isolated instance, love had triumphed over death, but Stafford's story resists such a pat interpretation. Its epiphanic conclusion instead dramatizes the paradox that such an idyllic relationship could, in effect, be spawned by a deathly ritual, a fact so inescapably horrifying that another American at the party, "snatching at the externals of the tale" (*CS*, 64), remarks on an antique guillotine he had once seen in Edinburgh, called the Maiden. Stafford thus conflates sexuality, love, and death as she dramatizes a bleak moment of psychological awareness in her innocent American's life that no doubt reflects her own cultural naïveté as a young woman in Heidelberg.

Jean Stafford's references to Heidelberg in these stories evoke a place redolent with memories for her, the first step away from the home she would unceasingly try to leave behind. As her sister Marjorie Stafford Pinkham wistfully notes in a reminiscence of Jean, "Jean was leaving home for good when she left for Heidelberg, and none of us ever lived under the same roof with her again."[16] The fellowship to study philology at the University of Heidelberg in 1936 introduced Stafford to an alien world preparing for war, and she was alternately seduced and repelled by what she saw. Later writings, such as "It's Good to Be Back" (1952) and "Souvenirs of Survival" (1960), document her naïveté and confusion as she lived the expatriate experience she had only read about. Her 1952 article "It's Good to Be Back" recapitulates the total immersion in experience the Heidelberg episode represented: "In a foreign country I know no leisure, for I am one of those visitors driven by a ravening and unselective greed for detail . . . and confronted at every turn by strangeness, I become a stranger to myself; my identity is suspended. . . . It is not until I am at home again and have calmed down and know where I am at that I can reflect and winnow, reduce, deduce, arrange."[17] Seduced by the picturesque town on the banks of the Neckar River, Jean drank in its Old World charm, keeping a journal of impressions for later years when she would use Heidelberg as the setting for such stories as "The Echo and the Nemesis" and "My Blithe, Sad Bird" and for her novella *A Winter's Tale*. Her literary apprenticeship had effectively begun.

One of the most powerful stories to come out of the Heidelberg experience, "The Echo and the Nemesis," originally titled "The Nemesis," appeared in the *New Yorker* in 1950.[18] A study of female friendship, obsessive behavior, and the dual self Kate Chopin articulates in *The Awakening*, it also explores the schizophrenic split Sandra Gilbert and Susan Gubar identify as characteristic of much writing by and about women.[19] This radical disunity in the female self consists of a public, conformist self and a private, subversive one expressing desires and appetites hidden from the world. Stafford's tale is the story of Sue Ledbetter and Ramona Dunn, Americans who are friends at the University of Heidelberg. Sue is naive, impressionable, and ordinary, while Ramona is overweight, intensely intellectual, and plagued with severe psychological problems. As the story unravels, the extent of Ramona's neurosis becomes painfully apparent. She invents a beautiful twin sister, Martha, who, Sue later discovers, is Ramona's former thin, beautiful self; tyrannizes Sue for her ordinariness; and ultimately retreats into her intellectuality, hurling insults at her frightened, escaping friend.

Certainly not typical *New Yorker* fare, the story echoes themes Stafford had dealt with earlier and on a larger canvas in her first novel, *Boston Adventure*, notably the friendship and rivalry between Sonie Marburg, a plain, socially respectable young woman, and Hopestill Mather, the beautiful, self-destructive, doomed rebel. Sonie yearns for the wealth and sophistication Hopestill represents, just as Sue covets the European breeding of Ramona and her family. This Heidelberg story reflects Stafford's own lifelong problems with alcohol, her anorexic tendencies, and the disfiguring automobile accident she survived in 1938 with Robert Lowell at the wheel. Stafford's numerous facial reconstructions could never approximate her once classically beautiful face; this traumatic incident no doubt accounts for her sensitive portrayals of female obsession with the body and aging.

Told through third-person narration, "The Echo and the Nemesis" was occasioned by Stafford's return to Germany and Heidelberg in 1949 and the inevitable confrontation she must have experienced between her present and former selves: the beautiful young woman she once was and the considerably changed Stafford of 10 years later. It also dramatizes other tensions Stafford felt in her life between solitude and society, intellectuality and domesticity, mind and body. Charlotte Goodman suggests that Stafford perhaps associates fatness with her anti-intellectual, domestic mother and thinness with her slight, intellectual father (28). Central to all of these themes is Stafford's preoccupation with identity: Sue vacillates between wanting to be a part of the students Ramona dismisses as Philistines and craving the detached, cerebral attitude Ramona evinces; Ramona constructs an impossibly romantic past for herself, complete with handsome, dissolute brothers, a beautiful mother, a dashing, philandering father, and a sickly, languishing sister who gazes soulfully out on the Riviera while playing the lute. Finally, these innocents abroad realize their common bond is their loneliness as the story leaves us to ponder the question Ann Hulbert formulates: "[Is] there any escape from this vision of life as a divided self, at once tyrant and victim, at the mercy of an unappeasable hunger for love?" (276).

Another Heidelberg story with an impressionable young woman as its focus is Stafford's 1954 novella, *A Winter's Tale*.[20] A bittersweet, first-person reminiscence by the 37-year-old Fanny about her student

red carpet thin and a "lugubrious puce [with] a vapid pattern of flaxen parallelograms" (*CS*, 20).

All of these unsavory details foreshadow her ultimate disillusionment when she discovers that Hugh is a part of this shadowy, lurid world and in thrall to it with an intensity he allows her to witness in order to prove any permanent relationship between them impossible. In the dingy, depressing Belgian casino, Abby is at first an outsider witnessing what is described almost as a secret ritual. She suffers the insolent stares of the gamblers, realizing that they resent her presence just as the gravely ill look longingly at the faces of the well. Finally, when she looks at Hugh's rapt absorption in the roulette game, she realizes she is uneasy, even jealous, though she is not sure of what. When Hugh describes his obsession to her, it becomes clear: "Eventually the only need you have in the world is the need to win. You don't need food or drink or sleep or sex—gamblers don't sleep with their wives . . . they sleep with numbers" (*CS*, 31).

Abby's revelation occurs at the end of the story when Hugh gently persuades her to try the roulette wheel. Initially inattentive and curious about the other gamblers, Abby gradually learns the rudiments of the game and begins winning heavily. The life and energy Stafford earlier refers to as missing from Abby's life since her husband's death return as a flushed and triumphant Abby, totally absorbed in the game, realizes with numbing clarity that "the wheel [had become] her quixotic lover, now scornfully rejecting her and now lavishly rewarding her" (*CS*, 32). Reality gradually asserts itself as the croupiers yawn, the tables empty, the noise lessens. In the final scene Abby leaves the site of this "children's game" and the man who now appears as insubstantial as "phantom ships" on the North Sea.

Two notably more lighthearted, comic stories appearing in the 1950s, Jean Stafford's most productive decade for short fiction, satirize what were painful experiences for the young Stafford. In both she achieves the comic distance that had eluded her in earlier novelistic attempts to deal with the same subjects. The first, "Maggie Meriwether's Rich Experience," dramatizes a young Nashville belle's first trip to Europe and how she navigates the treacheries and snobberies of a Paris garden party.[24] The second, "Caveat Emptor," is a withering look at Stafford's ill-fated experience teaching English at Stephens College in Missouri shortly after her graduation from college.[25]

The story of young Maggie Meriwether is a verbal tour de force whose sentences are sprinkled with foreign and obscure words and phrases, and whose tone is a masterful blending of the genteel and the colloquial. If, as Ann Hulbert maintains, its real subject is language, then it allows Stafford to both showcase her own stylistic quirks and see them as such (303). It also evokes Mark Twain's comic stylistic treatise "How to Tell a Story," which highlights the manner and not the matter of telling a tale.[26] Like Twain's piece, Stafford's story is a self-conscious examination of the craft by the crafter. Her heroine, miserably homesick and overdressed, finds herself "bamboozled into muteness by the language of France" (*CS*, 5), but she has her final victory as the story ends, with "the prettiest raconteur of middle Tennessee" (*CS*, 17) recounting her European adventure to sympathetic American friends. The story we have just read is Maggie's witty rendering of what could have been Edith Wharton's glacial social landscape but, recast in a comic vein, emerges as a minor misadventure in a young girl's life. Jean Stafford's comic muse triumphs in this brilliant short story.

A similar satiric foray, this time into the realms of academia, "Caveat Emptor" pokes fun not only at the Philistine environment of the Alma Hettrick College for Girls but also at its two new teachers, Malcolm and Victoria, pale and myopic from their research in philosophy and sixteenth-century English literature. Ill-suited to teach at this girls' finishing school, the two young scholars promptly find each other, fall in love, and escape on Sundays to a rural village not far from the university. On one level, as William Leary points out, the story is a romantic farce "played out against a mock-pastoral background whose occupants strikingly resemble the dramatis personae of a Gilbert & Sullivan operetta";[27] but the fact that Stafford changed its original innocuous title, "The Matchmakers," to the more menacing "Caveat Emptor" before including it in her *Collected Stories* suggests something deeper at work. Leary rightly notes the story's caustic gibes at just the kind of education Jean Stafford deplored: frivolous, anti-intellectual, and aimed at nothing more than pleasing the students and preparing them to become homemakers and society matrons. This clearinghouse for sorority girls, founded on a consumer ideology articulated by its president—"We are here to sell our girls Shakespeare and French and Home Economics and Ballet" (*CS*, 77)—becomes the target of Stafford's acerbic wit.

But the mellowing distance of almost 20 years allows the author to view herself through the double lens of Malcolm and Victoria, fresh from their arcane research much as Stafford was from her thesis on medieval love poetry. Stafford was definitely out of place among these wealthy, beautifully coiffed young women; someone at Stephens even suggested she go to the Grooming Clinic to pick up a few pointers. Her basic fears and insecurities as a new teacher, coupled with the gradual realization that she loathed teaching, resulted in the defensively ironic stance she took to the whole experience.

As in "Maggie Meriwether's Rich Experience," language provides the source of much of this story's humor. Throughout, Stafford cleverly mixes levels of diction to deepen contrasts: on their weekend excursions Malcolm parks his aging Buick in a "sylvan dingle"; he and Victoria fall in love over the Pernod and the crème brûlée and are promptly knocked "galley west" by the suddenness of the blow; they are both appalled by President Harvey's "pedagogical fiddlesticks." Faced with the onslaughts of twentieth-century life and the circuslike atmosphere of a progressive college, they seem curiously out of place.

The Bostonians and Other
Manifestations of the American Scene

While Jean Stafford's roots were in the West of her Colorado childhood, her adopted home and the locus of her early dreams of culture, breeding, and civilization was Boston and New England. This imaginative landscape appears in her first novel, *Boston Adventure* (1944); her last novel, *The Catherine Wheel* (1952); some of her finest short stories; and several of the brilliant nonfiction pieces she would write in the last decades of her life.

As she borrowed freely from Mark Twain, Jean also invoked Henry James in her choice of title for this segment of her short fiction. James dissected the American landscape he would ultimately abandon, just as Stafford would both admire and vilify New England and its rigid sensibilities. Time and again when we read Stafford's stories set in Boston or Maine, she seduces us with the weight and solidity of the objects that embellish an upper-class New England household: "damask tablecloths, Irish linen tea napkins, Florentine bureau runners, China silk blanket covers, point-lace doilies";[28] time and again we witness the emptiness beneath this facade of respectability. The qualities of intellectuality, breeding, and taste such objects seem to suggest are the very things Stafford could so virulently scorn.

But New England represented not only tradition, family structures, wealth, and power to Jean Stafford; it represented literary culture as well. Like Twain, who coveted the *Atlantic Monthly* milieu of William Dean Howells, Stafford equated a literary life with a New England setting. Before she married Robert Lowell, she settled herself in Concord, a town she called "a wonderful place for a lady writer,"[29] and made frequent visits to Sleepy Hollow Cemetery and the Louisa May Alcott house. Certainly, New England played a crucial part in Jean Stafford's unfolding literary identity—first as a youthful ideal and later, as it was for Sonie Marburg in *Boston Adventure*, an actual home. Her experiences helped her to flesh out this ideal, to penetrate its veneer, and to find that beneath it lurked the same passions and unfulfilled longings she found elsewhere. As part of her determined effort to remake herself and shed her undistinguished western background, Jean rarely returned to the West of her childhood except in fiction.

Boston and New England would never be a part of Jean Stafford's natural landscape, though she appropriated them for her own uses. Perhaps that is why with few exceptions the stories in this grouping are unrelievedly somber, peopled with lonely, orphaned young girls, some unhappily married, or bitter, frustrated old women. In some stories the setting is clearly delineated, as in "Polite Conversation," "A Country Love Story," "The Bleeding Heart," and "An Influx of Poets," while in others it is subtle and secondary to plot or character development, as in "The Interior Castle" and "Life Is No Abyss." Throughout these stories set in New England, Stafford's female characters seem to echo Sonie Marburg's haunting statement: "I was invaded by the strange feeling that I was not myself . . . that this was a phantom of myself, projected into Boston by my real being, still in Chichester."[30]

One of the most prominent locales in Stafford's short fiction is Damariscotta Mills, Maine, the site of her first house, bought in 1945 with the proceeds of her first novel. This remote village was the setting for a difficult period in Stafford's marriage to Robert Lowell, a period documented first in the lighthearted "Polite Conversation" and later in the bleaker stories "A Country Love Story" and "An Influx of Poets." The first of these stories, appearing in the *New Yorker* in 1949, was enthusiastically received by Katharine White, whose editorial comments include only relatively minor suggestions, such as dropping a reference to a radio show no longer current and clarifying the length of time the young couple in the story have been in the tiny village.

"Polite Conversation" focuses on a social ritual expected of new residents in this insular New England town—a teatime visit.[31] Margaret Heath visits Mrs. Wainwright-Lowe for tea while her husband stays home in his study to write. Margaret is a writer too, but her husband has foisted off all the social duties on her. The story recounts one such humorous duty call, based on Jean's actual experiences in Damariscotta Mills when Lowell casually left all the socializing to her while he remained isolated in his study. Stafford captures in this story the pointless, boring conversations she must have suffered through in order not to be labeled antisocial by the locals: talk of aristocratic family trees, inherited furniture, interior decorating schemes, flower gardens. Throughout, Mrs. Wainwright-Lowe, a bishop's widow with 11 children and an indefatigable social conscience, chastises Margaret for the isolated existence she and her husband have chosen and for their failure to join with the local Anglican community in its evangelical activities: "Margaret vividly recalled the scenes of January, when she and Tommy had been made to feel irresponsible and stonehearted because they would not give up their Saturdays to direct the games of sullen children who wholly hated this Christian intrusion upon their privacy" (*CS*, 126).

Yet beneath the idle banter lies a central tension in Stafford's and indeed any writer's life: between involvement with the world and withdrawal from it. Mrs. Wainwright-Lowe articulates the problem midway through the story when she maintains, "I think Tommy is gravely mistaken if he thinks one can live by art alone" (*CS*, 131). Margaret herself is ambivalent. On the one hand, she realizes the need to be a part of the intimate community of this isolated village; on the other, she loathes the bourgeois sound of the arguments she uses to persuade her recalcitrant husband to relent.

"A Country Love Story," which uses the remote New England setting to much bleaker ends, is generally regarded as one of Jean Stafford's finest stories.[32] This masterful portrait of a disintegrating relationship is firmly grounded in its wintry setting, complete with an antique sleigh that serves as focal point and symbol both for the leaden passing of time and for the inertia May and Daniel experience at this juncture in their married life.

May and Daniel suffer through a bitterly cold, isolating winter while Daniel, a university professor of history, recuperates from an illness. His doctor has ordered the solitude, but May yearns for some conversation and socializing. She and Daniel become increasingly estranged from each other until Daniel finally accuses her of madness and infidelity, and she, in retaliation, imagines a ghostly lover. This lover is her escape, her refuge, but one day she sees him sitting in the sleigh looking like an invalid. His identity and Daniel's merge as May wakes to Daniel's pleading with her to forgive him. The story ends with May resigned to her unchanging life, "like an orphan in solitary confinement" (*CS*, 145).

"A Country Love Story" treats the same theme of isolation versus immersion Stafford deals with in stories like "The Echo and the Nemesis" and "Polite Conversation." Thus, though the story is narrated primarily from a distant, detached third person point of view, we are sympathetically drawn into May's unstable world in passages like the following, which show multiple layers of consciousness at work: "But she did not disturb Daniel in his private musings; she held her tongue, and out of the corner of her eye she watched him watch the winter cloak the sleigh, and, as if she were computing a difficult sum in her head, she tried to puzzle out what it was that had stilled tongues that earlier, before Daniel's illness, had found the days too short to communicate all they were eager to say" (*CS*, 134).

Beneath the superficial seasonal references in this story lies an unmistakable sexual subtext. Moving in during the summer, May and Daniel are caught up not only with the beauty of the landscape and the architectural curves of their ancient farmhouse but with each other in what is "a second honeymoon." But as winter sets in with its long, dark silences, May remembers the doctor saying that "a long illness removes a thoughtful man from his fellow beings." It is, he says, "like living with an exacting mistress who is not content with half a man's attention but must claim it all" (*CS*, 135). Later, as the depth of their estrangement becomes apparent, May echoes the doctor's metaphor when she reflects that "to the thin, ill scholar whose scholarship and illness had usurped her place, she had gradually taken a weighty but unviolent dislike" (*CS*, 138).

Finally, when Daniel's accusations drive May to invent an imaginary lover who perversely consumes her thoughts and emotions, this lover assumes a primary role in the subversive subtext May creates for herself as she retreats into what must be sexual fantasies of this urbane, solicitous specter—fantasies that intrude when she is having tea with the neighborhood ladies, or buying groceries in the local store, "fearful that the old men loafing by the stove could see the incubus of her sins beside her" (*CS*, 141). During the day, when she goes to the barn for firewood she smells the earthy odor of horses once kept there and is reminded of "their passionate, sweating, running life" (*CS*, 139). At night "she lay straight beside [Daniel] as she slept . . . and tried not to think . . . of the man, her lover" (*CS*, 143).

This imaginary lover constitutes the subversive subtext early feminist critics such as Sandra Gilbert and Susan Gubar identify in texts by women writers (73). Undercutting the conventional text female characters often find themselves trapped in and mirroring their rebellious, hidden natures, such a rhetorical strategy often accompanies the heroine's painful awakening, as Susan Rosowski notes, to a profound acknowledgment of limitation.[33] Thus, May becomes increasingly introspective, lost in her musings, withdrawing into a world of her own creation when she finds the real world too frightening. Stafford reinforces this turning inward by the circular patterning of her narrative: the antique sleigh appearing in the first paragraph as a charming artifact of the past reappears at the conclusion in a more ominous light as May contemplates it and realizes that her life will not change. Though this somber realization saves her from madness, it also dooms her to a loveless sanity. She climbs into the sleigh, "hands locked tightly in her lap, rapidly wondering over and over again how she would live the rest of her life" (*CS*, 145).

Almost 30 years later Jean Stafford would return to this time in her life in one of the last stories to appear before her death in 1979. "An Influx of Poets" was extracted by her publisher Robert Giroux from her unfinished novel *The Parliament of Women*.[34] By making her heroine, Cora Savage Maybank, a teacher and not a writer, Stafford, even at the remove of 30 years, thereby avoids the issue of literary competition that plagued her marriage to Robert Lowell. Throughout the narrative, Stafford conflates the religious and the secular: Cora's doctor counsels her to "go and be shriven of [her] mortal sins by a psychoanalyst" ("Poets," 48); the Deep South cockroaches in Baton Rouge feast on the matched set of Cardinal Newman's works; and even the kindly Father Neuscheier, having chosen Baton Rouge as a perfect place to mortify the flesh, "[wears] the miasmas from the bayous like a hair shirt" ("Poets," 49). The religion of art to which Theron and his contemporary poets genuflect is its own exacting mistress, much like the peculiarly distorted Catholicism he invents, cast in the same mold as his Salem witch-burning ancestors. Cora, a victim of her domestic compulsions to decorate the first house she has ever owned, rationalizes by paralleling the adornment of churches to the enshrinement of marriage in its domestic temple. Clearly, these various obsessions—artistic, religious, domestic—cohere in this masterful short story.

Cora Maybank, the first-person narrator who wistfully evokes her past from a more mature, enlightened vantage point, is herself a portrait of the artist—imposing order on events that at the time seemed random and senseless. Like her creator, she has allowed events to sink in, impressions to germinate, before she can conjure them up in a structured narrative. In fact, the story functions as a kind of companion piece to the earlier "A Country Love Story" because it recalls some of the same events from a radically different perspective. The marriage, the fears of madness, the isolation, the retreat into domesticity—all emerge muted in this retrospective, remarkably self-aware narrative.

One of Stafford's earliest stories in this geographic grouping anticipates the later themes and styles she would develop. "The Interior Castle" appeared in the *Partisan Review* in 1946 and is the only attempt Jean Stafford made to fictionalize the automobile accident that permanently marred her face.[35]

Stafford's title is instructive. She chooses Saint Teresa of Avila's mystical work written in 1577, *Los Morados* (*The Dwelling Places*), which describes the soul's retreat through the seven-chambered interior castle of the soul. Teresa's contemplative piece gave Stafford a vehicle by which to convey the inexpressible—the excruciating physical and psychic pain occasioned by the actual surgery and its aftermath. Her heroine, Pansy Vanneman, retreats into the interior castle of her mind and remains aloof from the doctors and nurses who try to engage her in conversation. The doctor's proposed surgery will cut close to the brain, and the implications of this invasion resonate for Stafford's persona.

Unlike Teresa, Pansy contemplates not the soul but the brain, which she sees "now as a jewel, now as a flower, now as a light in a glass" (*CS*, 182) as she withdraws into some central core of self where she can be at peace. Stafford subverts religious mysticism, turning it to secular purposes, as she describes her heroine's reaching "the innermost chamber of [knowledge, which] . . . was the same as the saint's achievement of pure love" (*CS*, 182). Just as the mystic dreads the inevitable return to this world, Pansy fears the intrusive hand of the surgeon, who might maim her "treasure" and cause her either to die or to go mad: "While she did not question that in either eventuality her brain would after a time redeem its original impeccability, she did not quite yet wish to enter upon either kind of eternity, for she was not certain that she could carry with her her knowledge as well as its receptacle" (*CS*, 184).

In a savage perversion of a sacramental ritual, with unmistakable sexual overtones, Stafford describes the operation performed by Dr. Nicholas, who whispers to Pansy in "the voice of a lover," and Pansy's "ascent to the summit of something . . . a tower or a peak or Jacob's ladder" (*CS*, 189). She is left empty, hollowed out, "as dry as a white bone" (*CS*, 190). More than any other of Stafford's stories dealing with illness or disease, this one best captures the profound isolation of the stricken.

Lacking the clearly defined setting of the Damariscotta Mills stories, "The Interior Castle" nevertheless uses its wintry setting effectively as a fitting backdrop for the motionless passivity of Pansy Vanneman. Stafford pointedly contrasts outer and inner worlds—the "frozen river and leafless elm trees," "cold red brick buildings," "pale and inert" sky (*CS*, 180)—to the frozen immobility of Pansy's body and mind. Inner and outer worlds at one point seem to merge, "as if the room and the landscape, mortified by the ice, were extensions of herself" (*CS*, 181). Eerily premonitory of Stafford's young heroine Molly in her novel *The Mountain Lion* (published a year later, in 1947), who denies her sexuality and inflicts deliberate harm on herself, Pansy likewise seems to desire complete self-effacement as she prepares to subject herself to the surgeon's invasive knife.

Undeniably, "The Interior Castle" grimly dramatizes woman as object—to be poked, prodded, wondered and fantasized about (the nurses and attendants speculate about whether Pansy had been a beauty before her accident). Even Pansy's disconnected memories of her past life reinforce a sexual subtext: she remembers a veiled invitation to intimacy from one of her older male teachers; the old porter who wanders by her hospital room forms a "brutish word" with his "toothless mouth" (*CS*, 185). Pansy's brain—her treasure—is unmapped terrain implicitly analogous to her body. Stafford's language here is metaphorically rich: Pansy is "overwhelmed with the knowledge that the pain had been consummated in the vessel of her mind" (*CS*, 185). Perversely masochistic, Pansy sometimes invites the pain, "recklessly" desiring it "to attack her" (*CS*, 184). When the surgery is finally complete, she finds herself painfully aware of both inner and outer worlds—the first now "treasureless," the second promising a violent winter storm inescapably foreshadowing an uncertain future.

Two other stories set in New England and using a young woman as their locus of consciousness are "The Bleeding Heart" (1948) and "Life Is No Abyss" (1952). The earlier story particularizes the contrast between East and West that so fascinated Jean Stafford, while the later one focuses on the specter of old age as a complicating factor in the young woman's maturation.

"The Bleeding Heart" sets up its contrast between East and West in the first paragraph when we learn that Rose Fabrizio is a Mexican girl from the West transplanted to New England to work in a girls' boarding school as secretary to the headmistress.[36] Miss Talmadge misses no opportunity to remind Rose of her undistinguished origins, which she vaguely imagines connected to "cigar store Indians" and "clumps of sage" (*CS*, 147). The pristine setting of this small New England town (probably modeled on Concord, where Stafford briefly lived) entrances Rose as she compares its "venerable graveyards" and "imposing trees" to her barren, sterile western town, composed of dingy pool halls, beer parlors, and hotels whose windows were adorned with sweet potato vines planted in jam cans. In contrast, Rose notes that "the people here in this dignified New England town, shabby as they might be, wore hats and gloves at all hours . . . and appeared moral, self-controlled, well-bathed, and literate" (*CS*, 148).

Desperate to erase her childhood out West in a town largely Mexican, Rose constructs an alternative text for her life by secretly choosing as her foster father a handsome, distinguished man she sees in the library. Her real parents are still alive, but her memories of them—especially of her "stupid," "cynical" unwashed father in his army surplus clothes—are bitter and spiteful. Rejecting her shabby past and embracing what she feels is a much more desirable present, Rose dreams of adoption and tries to remake herself in the image of a proper New England daughter. She reads Emerson's "Self-Reliance" to soothe her restless spirit.

Predictably, illusion and reality meet in the second half of the story when Rose delivers a bleeding heart plant from the headmistress to a sick old woman and discovers that this woman's unmarried son is her romanticized foster father. In a macabre sickroom scene replete with an obscene, squawking parrot, a senile, embittered old woman who can only communicate in nouns and pronouns—"Tea!" "Toast!" "Me!"—and her leering, pathetic son, Stafford evokes a family dynamic as grotesque as Rose's own. With deft touches she describes a grim parody of a New England tea, worlds away from Rose's dreams of lace doilies and aristocratic interiors: "On the tray were a plate of English muffins and a jar of peanut butter and one of marmalade and a store-bought pound cake and a dish of pickled peaches. There were a can of evaporated milk and a tin of bouillon cubes" (*CS*, 165). As the old woman drinks bouillon she thinks is tea, Rose wonders how and if she will ever be able to forget this scene of naked loneliness. She rejects Mr. Benson's pitiful attempt to have her call him "Daddy," aware that the relationship he proposes is not the parental one she had desired. In the last scene Stafford has Benson reveal to Rose that his yellow silk ascot hides an ugly wen.

Seeking to authenticate herself, Rose Fabrizio is one of Stafford's lonely, alienated young women—reminiscent of Sonie Marburg in *Boston Adventure*—who imagine a radically different life for themselves and are inevitably disappointed. Jean Stafford looked old age, illness, and death squarely in the face and gave them imaginative power in her short fiction.

Another look at old age and its afflictions, "Life Is No Abyss" takes place within the walls of a New England nursing home in a muted winter landscape.[37] But though its external landscape remains hazy, this story lays bare the aristocratic pretensions and mindless prejudices of Isobel Carpenter, the Boston octogenarian who claims to have been incarcerated by her Cousin Will in this shabby poorhouse. Her 20-year-old orphaned Cousin Lily visits one day, taking Will's place, and the ensuing confrontation between youth and old age takes place.

Reveling in her self-imposed martyrdom, Isobel is an inveterate snob, icily class-conscious, who passes judgment on the grim public institution, the doctors, the food—but most bitingly on her less fortunate inmates and their various afflictions. She is merciless as she makes the poorhouse a microcosmic representation of the decidedly hierarchical world she was born into. She separates herself from "the others" who rave, moan, babble, and eventually die, while Lily remembers her Cousin Isobel in happier days, when Isobel's father, Judge Carpenter, was alive and they lived in splendor in an elegant North Shore summer home.

What Lily sees as well are images of twisted, deformed old age that seem to mock her youth and beauty: "Lily could see into the large ward, where every bed . . . was occupied by an ancient, twisted woman; the humps of their withered bodies under the seersucker coverlets looked truncated and deformed like amputated limbs or mounds of broken bones, and the wintry faces that stared from the stingy pillows had lost particularity. . . . [A]ge and humiliation . . . had all but erased the countenance" (*CS*, 101). Like Rose Fabrizio, or Fanny in *A Winter's Tale*, Lily has a sobering vision of what the future may hold for her, as she witnesses from a comfortable distance the bitterness and isolation of old age. Her errand of mercy has brought her face to face with poverty, disease, and dementia—a spectacle played out against the hauntingly ironic refrain of "Life Is No Abyss," a popular song blaring from a nearby radio. The story ends with Lily feeling isolated not only by her youth but by her failure to see how and why this family, as her Cousin Augusta protests, can still love the embittered old woman who refuses to be rescued from her prison. "Repudiat[ing] her hypocritical family blood" (*CS*, 112), Lily gratefully escapes into the arms of her waiting boyfriend.

In a *Holiday* magazine essay called "New England Winter," written two years after "Life Is No Abyss," Jean Stafford describes the stern beauty of a New England winter and evokes both its rigors and its blessings. Significantly, she relates this frozen landscape to "the adversities and tribulations" of the Pilgrims of 300 years ago, thus placing her recurring setting in an explicit historical context.[38] Jean's descriptions of the isolating winters in Damariscotta become emblematic of the disenchantment all such visions ultimately suffer. Her modern-day pilgrims seem to live in a world similarly threatening and unknown— fated to fall short of their illusions.

Cowboys and Indians, and Magic Mountains

Though Jean Stafford adopted other geographic regions as her own, the West of her childhood and adolescence formed the background for the majority of her short stories. Jean spent the first six years of her life in California, but her father's unwise financial decisions caused the family to relocate to Boulder, where she spent the remainder of her childhood and young adult years. This journey from California to Colorado served as the subject for her first published essay, written at age 15 and appearing in the Boulder *Daily Camera*. Titled "Disenchantment," the essay anticipates the more mature Stafford in both subject matter and style, as it deflates the family's romantic dreams of adventure in Colorado while assuming the Twainian narrative persona of *Roughing It*. As Ann Hulbert maintains, Twain's rough-edged travel narrative lies behind Stafford's youthful piece (17).

As Stafford mapped this childhood terrain in her western stories, Boulder became Adams, Colorado—an Edenic place whose name conjures up images of primal innocence and a fall from grace. Like Faulkner's Yoknapatawpha or Anderson's Winesburg, Adams assumes mythic proportions for Stafford and her readers, for it evokes an imaginative landscape we all share. Eudora Welty asserts about these places of our youth, "There may come to be new places in our lives that are second spiritual homes—closer to us in some ways, perhaps, than our original homes. But the home tie is the blood tie. And had it meant nothing to us, any place thereafter would have meant less, and we would carry no compass inside ourselves to find home ever, anywhere at all."[39] Near the end of her life, Jean Stafford echoes these words in the prefatory "Author's Note" to her *Collected Stories*, maintaining that her "roots remain in the semi-fictitious town of Adams, Colorado, although [she] . . . may abide in the South or the Midwest or New England or New York," a surprising admission from the writer who confessed to "leaving home" at age seven. The same impulse that drove her to seek surrogate homes and surrogate parents

30

inevitably brought her back—imaginatively, at least—to the West of her childhood.

As with Henry James, Stafford's prefaces are revealing. In this introduction to a compilation of her best work, she not only asserts her geographic roots but also establishes a complex literary heritage: her father's ill-fated western novel, *When Cattle Kingdom Fell*, and her cousin Margaret's feminized view of the West, *A Stepdaughter of the Prairie*— neither of which she claims to have read. But by imaginatively situating herself in relation to these two diverse images of the West—what she called the "wicked" and the "noble" West—Stafford is also articulating what later feminist critics such as Elaine Showalter have identified as the woman writer's dual heritage. In "Feminist Criticism in the Wilderness," Showalter speaks of women writers confronting both "paternal and maternal precursors," being "not inside and outside of the male tradition" but "inside two traditions simultaneously."[40] More specific to Stafford's western stories, critics like Susan Armitage and Annette Kolodny have distinguished between a male and a female West—the one stereotypically linked with space, adventure, and passion; the other with domestic spaces, nurturing, and creativity.[41] But as Stafford admits in the "Author's Note" to *Collected Stories*, by the time she began writing neither of these two heroic Wests existed. In their place was a sanitized, tamed-down landscape full of dandies from the East and leftovers from the glory days. In *The Mountain Lion*, her most extended treatment of the western theme, Stafford demythologizes the West by making it the locus of distinctly unheroic actions and frequently comparing it to the East, that other frontier of the American consciousness—to the detriment of both. In Stafford's fiction, then, the West emerges not just as a geographic region but perhaps more importantly as a complex of attitudes and assumptions that gave her a way of mocking not only the East of her childhood dreams but also the West itself.

Jean's later comments on the rugged contours of the West illuminate a landscape she often found threatening and alien. In a 1950 essay called "Enchanted Island," she contrasts the island topography to the mountainous terrain she knew as a child, asserting that she found the Rocky Mountains "too big to take in, too high to understand, too domineering to love." She goes on to articulate her impassioned attempt to tame this landscape and "to reduce the world to a rational arena where I knew, at all times, what was going on."[42] Because Stafford is intimidated by the stark, forbidding mountains and prairies, she must, like her heroine Molly in *The Mountain Lion*, find a way to tame and domesticate what is so frightening and inhospitable. The comic voice of her childhood narrators and her skillful manipulation of both formal and colloquial diction in some of the western stories represent Stafford's way of taming the difficult terrain of her past.

Typically, the girls and women in Stafford's fictional western world test the limits of what Melody Graulich describes as the "rigid sex roles" imposed by the West,[43] rebelling against conventions and traditions they consider inhibiting. Yet not surprisingly, it is her younger heroines like Emily Vanderpool who are most successful in their rebellions. When we encounter older versions of these independent, feisty girls, they are resigned, beaten down by experience, and more like the passive victims we see elsewhere in Stafford's fictional world. Daisy and her sister in Stafford's prizewinning "In the Zoo" (1953) are mere shadows compared to their youthful counterpart Emily. Stafford's ambivalence toward the West effectively subverts the frontier myth animating so much of American literature: her heroines, past childhood, rarely have a chance to start over. Instead, they compromise, accommodate, and simply accept the confinements of a life remembered against what seems to them the inhuman landscape of the West.

Stafford's first published story, "And Lots of Solid Color" (1939),[44] takes place in a western setting, and while a slight piece, it foreshadows several themes that would haunt Stafford as she matured artistically: the problematic influence of her writer-father, her own insecurities as a writer, and the desire for a real home as an antidote to her boarding-house existence in Colorado. The story documents one painful day in a young woman's life as she waits for the mail to come and bring her news of a job. A recent college graduate, Marie lives in Oregon with her parents and an embittered, carping old aunt who makes snide references to her niece's college education. Marie's father, like Stafford's own, is a writer who also anxiously awaits the mail for the one acceptance that will make him and his family rich. He has been waiting for 15 years.

Marie views her pathetic father with ironic detachment as she sees her own fate mirrored in his patient waiting: "His flesh was melting away as he sat hour after hour at his typewriter quarrelling with Marx and Roosevelt, Christ and hundreds of others grouped into the general category of 'abstractionists.' His eyes were red from strain behind glasses that were wrong and could not be replaced" ("Color," 24). Her failure to find a job—even as a photographer's model—makes her fear a life of trying to "live on words as her father had done all his life" ("Color," 23). But an equally disturbing premonition of her future is Aunt Eva, the bent, withered old spinster who has come to live out the rest of her life with Marie's family. These images of a stunted old age cause Marie to dream of an adobe house in Mexico—a place she remembers vividly—filled with "lots of solid color pottery dishes and Mexican blue glassware" ("Color," 24)—and with supportive, admiring friends. The story ends with yet another job rejection and with Aunt Eva's spiteful commentary on the uselessness of a college education.

Aunt Eva's final comments perhaps echo Stafford's own feelings at this time in her life when, back from Heidelberg, she was preparing for a career and "preoccupied with the question of reconciling domestic, practical values and intellectual, artistic aspirations" (Hulbert, 73). Reinforcing this tension, the straightforward, chronological narrative contains passages of Marie's interior monologue where she rehashes bits and pieces of rejection letters, her father's pointless ramblings, and accusatory letters from her family citing her lack of responsibility and hopeless dreams. Interestingly, Marie's domestic dreams include not the aristocratic yearnings of Stafford's later heroines, such as Sonie Marburg in *Boston Adventure*, but the less pretentious vision of a Mexican adobe house decorated in bright primary colors.

Jean Stafford's second published story, "The Darkening Moon" (1944),[45] treats a similarly bleak theme but seen through the eyes of a younger heroine. Here Stafford introduces the innocent child figure that would appear in many of her best stories and foregrounds the western landscape she would use so brilliantly three years later in *The Mountain Lion*. Mary Ellen Williams Walsh sees this story as "emblematic of Stafford's portrayal of the young girl in the West" in its pointed divergence from a typical male questing journey.[46] Rather than a world of infinite possibility and fulfillment, Stafford's fatherless heroine Ella sees only a threatening landscape and an uncertain destination as she travels through the western dark, symbolizing her transition from childhood to adolescence. In its downward spiral Ella's journey also reflects the typical pattern of the female initiation story identified by such critics as Susan Rosowski, a pattern involving not movement outward to a welcoming world but movement inward to an acceptance of limitation (Rosowski, 49).[47] In "The Darkening Moon" Stafford in fact seems to be establishing the paradigm of female development that would figure in most of her works: a growth into disillusionment, constriction, and uncertainty.

Part 1

The story concerns a 12-year-old girl's nighttime journey on her brother's horse Squaw to babysit for family friends, the Temples. It is a journey Ella has made before and will make again, and contrary to reader expectations, she is frightened not as she is riding toward her destination amid the howls of bobcats and coyotes but only when she arrives at the Temple house and closes herself up within its walls. Ella's father, before his death, had taught her not to fear nature and the dark, and this particular night she remembers his lesson wistfully: "So long as she was outdoors, she was not afraid at night. Her father had taught her that, long ago, when she was only a little girl of five and he had taken her and Fred fishing one night when the grayling were spawning. They had left her alone at the riverbank for half an hour while they went upstream through brush that would have cut her bare legs. Before they left, her father had said, 'There ain't nothing to harm you, sister. The animals is all there is and they won't be looking you up' " (*CS*, 254). But the landscape Ella travels through is not completely without danger, for she must contend with a skittish mare who bolts at a full moon, at the sight of the bluffs on either side of the highway, or at the sound of the Santa Fe Trailways bus. As she makes her way through the uncertain darkness, Ella remembers her previous trips when, arriving at the Temple house, she would sit rigid in a high wingback chair, listening to the outside noises and staring at the painting of the Temples' prize bull on the opposite wall.

From the beginning of the story, Stafford clearly delineates Ella's journey as archetypically female by calling attention to the male images framing it. She rides her brother's horse—appropriately named Squaw; she notes how her brother's voice has taken on the cadences of their dead father's—a fact Ella finds disturbing; she imagines her brother's male talk tonight at Uncle Joe's with his friends, boasting of the "six-point buck" someone shot. Later, after Ella reaches the Temple house, she hears the noise of Squaw being kicked by Mr. Temple's horse, a "big, mean, ball-faced black" (*CS*, 257). Ella even remembers a fishing trip with her father when she had plunged into the cold, slimy water amid the clammy fish and "he had smeared her wrist with fish's blood which dripped in gouts from his fingertips as if it were his own" (*CS*, 261). The "horror of the reptilian odor" (*CS*, 261) still haunts her. Presiding over all Ella's reminiscences is the red-ringed moon, emblematically female, which gradually diminishes as the story unravels.

When the Temples return to the shaken Ella, Mrs. Temple empathizes with the young girl and solemnly reflects on her own amorphous adolescent fears: "Some way, as you get older . . . I don't know. I'm just thinking the way I used to be. Until I was fifteen, wasn't a living thing could give me a turn. And then, later on . . ." (*CS*, 262). Stafford's narrative thus achieves a tentative closure, a circularity emphasizing not the linear progress of a charmed hero but the repetitive, inward-turning movement of a disenchanted heroine. Ella's journey takes her back on a known path now suddenly defamiliarized: "A world slipped past her blinded eyes as she traversed a road she would not recognize again, beneath the full, unfaithful moon" (*CS*, 262).

Both of these rather somber early Stafford stories set in the West are told by an omniscient narrator with a detached, objective angle of vision appropriate for the abstract nature of the fictional material: a young woman's painful confrontation with an unloving, unreceptive world; a young girl's mythic journey from childhood to adolescence. Stafford had not yet mined the innocent eye technique of the childhood narrator—she had not yet found the authentic voice—that served her mentor Mark Twain so well in *Huckleberry Finn*. But as she developed her literary aesthetic, Jean Stafford would formulate a new critical philosophy connecting the childhood world she evokes so powerfully with the ironic technique she uses to depict it.

In a 1952 interview with Alice Dixon Bond in the *Boston Sunday Herald*, appearing when Stafford was writing her childhood stories with western settings, she clarifies both her choice of subject matter and her technique. Normally reticent about framing an artistic credo, Stafford is unusually forthright in this discussion as she admits that "the impact of her own frustrations and sufferings engendered by her childhood . . . has illumined her understanding and deepened her compassion for . . . children."[48] She goes on to articulate a belief that animates the best of her fiction: "My theory about children is my theory about writing. The most important thing in writing is irony, and we find irony most clearly in children. The very innocence of a child is irony. Irony, I feel, is a very high form of morality" (Bond, n.p.).

The first of the Adams, Colorado, stories, "The Healthiest Girl in Town" (1951),[49] introduces a child narrator, Jessie, who foreshadows the Emily Vanderpool narrator of "Bad Characters," "A Reading Problem," and "The Scarlet Letter." This series of western stories, all told in the first person, represents what Stafford biographer David Roberts calls "the zenith of Stafford's career as a writer of short fiction."[50] During the same period when Stafford's stories of adult alienation, such as "The Echo and the Nemesis" or "A Country Love Story," were appearing, she was also writing these stories of youthful loneliness and rebellion tempered by the comic voice of her childhood narrators. Imaginatively returning to the Boulder of her early years, Jean Stafford vividly re-created it as a fitting backdrop for the escapades of her rebellious young heroines. Her eye for the telling detail and her ear for the rough colloquialisms of westerners combined to evoke a cross-section of humanity worthy of Huck Finn's ride down the river. As David Roberts notes, "Never had Stafford realized and reinvented a town and its inmates more acutely than she now did Boulder: all of her childhood jaunts to the dump, to the top of the mesa, to the hobo shantytown of the 'Jungle' came back to her, allowing her to flesh out a Colorado town that is like nothing in the history books" (312).

One of Stafford's fatherless heroines, Jessie tells the story of her relationship to two ailing schoolmates from the East, the Butler girls, who act socially superior to her not only because they are from Massachusetts but also because they are afflicted with a variety of illnesses that, in this town of convalescing tuberculars, marks them for distinction. (The Boulder of Stafford's youth was in fact the site of a sanitarium for recovering tuberculosis patients from the East and the South, and Charlotte Goodman notes that Jean remembered hearing their coughs and muted voices as she and her siblings walked through their neighborhood streets.) Jessie's mother is a nurse for the Butler family, and this fact adds to her feelings of embarrassment and isolation. The Butler girls taunt Jessie for her rustic ways and good health until finally, in a fit of desperation to impress them, she tells the girls her father died of leprosy. Predictably, this story serves not to ingratiate her with the afflicted but to isolate her even more. Ultimately forced to tell the truth, Jessie sees the Butler girls for what they are—weak-eyed, pitiful snobs—and she exults in being the healthiest girl in town.

Thematically, this story is vintage Stafford. An atmosphere of disease and illness, a shadowy father figure, a lonely, socially self-conscious young girl, a rugged West pitted against an effete East—all combine to create the story of a young girl's temporary triumph over a constricting environment. What distinguishes "The Healthiest Girl in Town" is its portrayal of a hierarchy of illness, a social stratification every bit as rigid as the one Jessie observes in the larger world. The wealthy tuberculars live in the Swiss chalet sanitarium resembling a resort, where they play bridge and mah-jongg and photograph the breathtaking mountain scenery. To Jessie, despite their affliction, they have a glamorous air, for as she reflects, they "had the solaces of money and of education . . . and could hire cars to go driving in the mountains" (*CS*, 199–200). At the other extreme of the social spectrum are the "indigent tuberculars," who live in run-down cottages at the edge of town, "sputum cups on the windowsills" (*CS*, 200). These invalids inspire pity in Jessie, for in their patient, monotonous coughing she hears a profound weariness with life and a resignation to their fate. Between these two extremes are the solid middle-class patients, who live in houses much like those they left behind in Virginia or Connecticut and who are homesick for family and friends. Laura and Ada Butler and their parents belong to this group, and besides their illnesses, what adds to Jessie's feeling of isolation from them is the fact that the wages her mother earns as their nurse pay for Jessie's one luxury—dancing class. Thus, she is doubly alienated: by health and by social class. Disease in this story thus becomes simply another class indicator.

Stafford further reinforces Jessie's plight by contrasting the Boston world of the transplanted Butlers to their rugged western surroundings. With the painful self-consciousness of the young, Jessie notes all the trappings of their transplanted eastern way of life, from the Oriental rugs and framed family portraits to the "Boston accents and adult vocabularies" (*CS*, 203) of these two miniature adults. Mrs. Butler too is clearly out of place in Adams, and as Jessie wryly notes, "[she] had an orthodox aversion to the West, and although almost no one was native to our town, she looked down her pointed nose at the entire population" (*CS*, 205). Throughout the passages contrasting East and West, Stafford cleverly mixes levels of diction to emphasize the disparity between Jessie's ordinary childhood world out West and the Butlers' unnaturally adult one back East: rather than normal children's games, "at the Butlers' house the only divertissements were Authors and I Spy, and it was only once in a blue moon that we played those" (*CS*, 204); rather than the spirited give and take of childhood talks, Jessie remembers that "the Butler girls were dauntlessly opinionated and called the tune to me, who supinely took it up" (*CS*, 204). Inevitably, the Butlers' world temporarily seduces Jessie and causes her to internalize all of their criticisms of what she perceives as her shamelessly healthy, relentlessly ordinary lower-class life.

Finally rejecting the tyrannies of language and social class the Butlers inflict, Jessie admits to lying about her father's leprosy and, in doing so, realizes her power over these pale, sickly girls across whose "small, old faces there flickered a ray of curiosity to know, perhaps, how the other half lived" (*CS*, 216). Her breezy goodbye—"So long, kids, see you in church" (*CS*, 216)—represents a final triumph over the "children" who do not talk but "converse," and who call their lunch a "light collation." Stafford's editor at the *New Yorker*, Katharine White, had in fact suggested such an ending for the story, believing that Jessie's confession and final acceptance of her good health would strengthen it (Davis, 160). The final version of the story reflects these changes.

Jessie's exchanges with the Butler girls clearly reflect Stafford's own profound self-consciousness about her western origins. But the exuberant ending of "The Healthiest Girl in Town" also reflects another attitude—one Stafford's friend Howard Moss notes in his remembrance of Jean after her death: "She was a special mixture of the outlandish and the decorous. She paid great respect to the civilized, but something ingrained and Western in her mocked it at the same time. Think of Henry James being brought up in Colorado."[51]

During 1952–59 Jean Stafford produced a group of short stories set in Adams and introducing her comic persona Emily Vanderpool. All narrated from the first-person point of view—one by Tess Vanderpool, Emily's sister, and the others by Emily herself—these stories focus on a young girl who cultivates her outlaw status within the confines society has prescribed. She rebels against traditions and conventions, but she is basically harmless. In fact, Stafford, in the "Author's Note" to her 1964 collection of short stories, *Bad Characters*, characterizes Emily as a "bad character" who is as much a victim as a perpetrator of misdeeds. Stafford also specifically identifies herself as a young girl with her character Emily: "[She] is someone I knew well as a child; indeed, I often occupied her skin and, looking back, I think that while she was notional and stubborn and a trial to her kin, her talent for iniquity was feeble" (BC, vii). Clever, restless, and literary like the young Stafford, Emily lives in a tamed-down, bourgeois West offering little opportunity for adventure, and so the impressionable young girl often creates her own excitement—by constructing imaginary stories to scare her younger sister, or by hooking up with the itinerant, unsavory characters who pass through Adams.

We first meet Emily through her sister Tess in the 1952 story "The Violet Rock."[52] Like the other Emily Vanderpool stories, "The Violet Rock" fleshes out a portrait of the artist as a young girl out West—brainy, volatile, and imaginatively stifled. Feeling powerless in the larger world, Emily rebels against her immediate surroundings, throws tantrums, and inspires awe and fear in her younger sister, who becomes the object of Emily's frequent rages. Since Adams bears faint resemblance to the abode of desperadoes and gun-toting cowboys with steely blue eyes, Emily as budding artist must create a heroic text out of the materials at hand. To frighten Tess, she constructs an imaginary story concerning Mr. Norman Ferris, a polo-playing easterner and wealthy owner of the Gold Palace Hotel. Ferris, according to Emily, remembers the day Tess "sassed" him—called him a "dude"—and he has vowed revenge. Presumably, he and his mad scientists have injected the violet rock looming up in the mountains with gentian violet, a lethal gas that is released only at twilight and directed solely at Tess.

Though Tess narrates, it is clearly Emily who directs the narrative. Like Molly in *The Mountain Lion*, Emily is often a creature possessed, and her possession always involves language. In her milder, literary moments, she wanders the mesas with her sister, reciting Wordsworth's "I wandered lonely as a cloud"; in her wilder moods, she invents ghost stories and "tales of mutilation and kidnapping" ("Rock," 35) or hurls curses at randomly targeted acquaintances while doing bizarre, gesticulating dances. Her tone, Tess notes, "ranged from the iciest sarcasm to the fieriest venom" ("Rock," 36). Emily's innately self-dramatizing tendency often results in stories so powerful they can cast a strange and lurid light on a once loved and familiar scene. As Tess reflects, "I knew every inch of the park by heart—each tree and turning, each boulder and minuscule plot of grass. . . . But this evening, as I glanced away from Emily, the whole place looked altogether unfamiliar to me, unnaturally dark, the cottonwoods immense, and the springtime voice of the creek that bifurcated it was strange" ("Rock," 36).

But the spell of language the imaginative Emily casts on this familiar landscape suggests something more than sibling tyranny. What the story describes—through comparing Emily to Svengali and Tess to Trilby ("Rock," 37)—is the process of narrative seduction at the heart of the storyteller's art. Words skillfully wielded have enormous power: the lichen-covered boulder Tess and her brother Jack routinely play on becomes, through Emily's verbal machinations, a violet rock seething with lethal gas and intended as the agent of Tess's destruction.

Emily Vanderpool's love affair with language recalls Jean Stafford's own early passion for words, fueled by her parents' tales of their childhood adventures and family history. Conscious of her father's cowpunching western roots and her mother's more proper, blue-blooded heritage, the young Stafford invariably found the legends of her paternal cowboy grandfather more intriguing. Her novel *The Mountain Lion* treats a similar family dynamic, when Ralph and Molly feel they must choose between Grandfather Bonney's aristocratic pretensions and Grandpa Kenyon's tales of meeting Jesse James. But John Stafford himself was also a curious mix of these two impulses: his bookshelves contained Ovid, Virgil, Shakespeare, and Mark Twain; his western tales often flaunted such incongruous titles as "The Transmogrified Calf." Clearly, the impressionable young Jean absorbed this complex literary heritage and used it to advantage in stories like "The Violet Rock" that reflect the narrative seductions of her youth.

Always concerned with precision and clarity in language, Stafford was equally attuned to nuances of diction and style and to regional variations in usage. She had an ear for the telling phrase, the offbeat metaphor, the colorful analogy. In her travels through the United States, she would frequently jot down in her journals words and phrases that would later appear in her stories and novels and in her conversation, which was sprinkled with a strange mixture of the literary and the colloquial. Two of her favorite expressions were "in a pig's valise" and "it's none of your beeswax"—both worthy of her character Lotty Jump, who so enthralls Emily Vanderpool in the story "Bad Characters." In her later years Stafford would deride the homogenization of the English language, blaming television and the movies for their insidious influence. In a 1973 essay, "Plight of the American Language," she laments this inevitable process in a comment that sheds light on her western tales: "[W]hat is going to become of regional speech? Who will carry on the rich oral traditions of New England and the South and the West? I reckon that convicts and children, who have the most time on their hands, will go on contriving slang and jokes, and, God willing, the wellspring will not be polluted and will not go dry, and hillbillies and pickpockets and able-bodied seamen and timbercruisers and southern politicians will go on sweetening the pot."[53]

Near the end of "The Violet Rock," when young Tess finally makes her peace with Mr. Ferris by telling her version of Emily's treacheries, Ferris is obviously curious about the kind of girl who could concoct such an outlandish tale and have such power over her younger sister. As he banishes the "spell" he has supposedly placed on Tess and hands her a silver dollar to seal the bargain, his last words are "I'll be interested to know what ever becomes of Emily" ("Rock," 42). Her story—even as retold by Tess—retains its imaginative allure.

Two years after Tess and Emily's story appeared in the *New Yorker*, Jean Stafford allowed Emily to tell her own story in the prizewinning "Bad Characters" (1954).[54] The title story of Stafford's third collection of short stories, "Bad Characters" is the story of Emily's encounter with the incorrigible Lottie Jump, whose "only recreation and . . . only gift was . . . stealing" (*CS*, 266). The resolutely amoral Lottie plans an excursion to the five-and-dime, where her dutiful pupil Emily is caught shoplifting. Lottie plays deaf and dumb, Emily has to take the blame, and the story ends with Emily vowing to control her lawless enthusiasms and her tongue.

Emily's avowed predilection for swearing—what she calls her "awful tongue" (*CS*, 263)—introduces the story, brings about its conclusion, and forms its thematic center. From the first paragraph Stafford foregrounds language and sets the stage for Emily's inevitable entrapment by the word-wielding Lottie. Emily first sees Lottie stealing a freshly baked chocolate cake from Mrs. Vanderpool's kitchen. Her quickly thought-out response when Emily discovers her trespassing is "I came to see if you'd like to play with me" (*CS*, 265), an answer so blatantly false that it immediately wins over the lonely, bad-tempered Emily. Lottie laughs violently at the ridiculous name Emily Vanderpool, causing the gullible Emily to look at herself through considerably less favorable eyes. But when Lottie tells her improbable life story to the enraptured Emily, her triumph is complete.

Lottie's questionable family saga is as unsavory and antiestablishment as Emily's is staunchly bourgeois and respectable. The daughter of a tuberculosis-ridden railroad man and a half-Indian mother, Lottie lives with her parents and an illiterate brother in a shanty village; she hates school, loves snakes, and thinks Adams is a "slowpoke town," a "one-horse burg" (*CS*, 268). Seduced by her "gaudy, cynical talk" (*CS*, 268), Emily hangs on every word and is an easy mark for Lottie's shoplifting excursion. In this classic confrontation between innocence and experience, the narrator, Emily, examines her previously staid, predictable life and realizes it has been "deadly prim; all I'd ever done to vary the monotony of it was to swear" (*CS*, 269). Her desire for Lottie's friendship wins out over her moral sense, and she agrees to accompany Lottie on a shoplifting spree the following Saturday.

In passages reminiscent of Huck Finn's moral deliberations, Emily watches her family's reaction to her increasing nervousness as Saturday approaches: "And because I was the cause of it all and my conscience was after me with red-hot pokers, I finally *had* to have a tantrum" (*CS*, 271). Lottie's rhetoric has seduced Emily, and even before the Saturday assignation she is forced to commit minor crimes, such as inventing an imaginary hobo who stole the chocolate cake and breaking into her

Sunday school bank to get trolley fare. Midway through the story Emily confesses, "I had a bad character, I know that, but my badness never gave me half the enjoyment Jack and Stella thought it did. A good deal of the time I wanted to eat lye" (*CS*, 274). She further castigates herself by admitting she never wanted to see Lottie Jump again, even though she had been entranced by her "style of talking and the expert way she had made off with the perfume flask and the cake" (*CS*, 274). Contemplating the probable effects of her proposed lawless adventure, Emily concludes that "the part of me that did not love God was a black-hearted villain" (*CS*, 274).

Like Huck Finn's irresistible attraction to Tom Sawyer, Emily's attraction to Lottie centers on her boldness and her seeming indifference to consequences. Emily is drawn to Lottie's disreputable status; but in the end, the shoplifting spree becomes as pointless as Tom's romantically conceived plot to free Jim. Seen without regard to the larger world, both Lottie and Tom seem to confer a kind of glamour on the gullible Emily and Huck. As Emily reflects near the climax of the story, "But in another way I *was* proud to be with her; in a smaller hemisphere, in one that included only her and me, I was swaggering— I felt like Somebody, marching along beside this lofty Somebody from Oklahoma who was going to hold up the dime store" (*CS*, 278). But examined more closely, their exploits seem random acts performed without reflection—reckless and self-gratifying.

Throughout Stafford's narrative, the comic voice of Emily Vanderpool alternates with the mature, reflective comments of the older, wiser Emily; the result is a wry, ironic fable with a clearly recognizable villain and an innocent victim. As Emily remembers her childhood nemesis, she reflects on her probable whereabouts: "I don't know where Lottie is now—whether she is on the stage or in jail. If her performance after our arrest meant anything, the first is quite as likely as the second" (*CS*, 281). Subjected to a sermon by her father's friend Judge Bay, to her mother's tearful remarks that she had "nurtured an outlaw" (*CS*, 282), and to numerous goading comments from Jack and Stella, Emily repents and reforms if for no other reason than a pragmatic one. She is ultimately welcomed into the Camp Fire Girls, sheds her outlaw status, and becomes thoroughly civilized and respectable.

The third and last Emily Vanderpool story to appear in the *New Yorker* was "A Reading Problem" (1956).[55] Like "Bad Characters," it depicts Emily at odds with her environment: with her family, because her mother interrupts her reading to urge her to sit near a light or to go out and play so she'll get roses in her cheeks, and with her town, because except in the fall Adams and its harsh mountain climate are not conducive to reading outside. The library is off limits, because her dog Reddy often follows her there and once scared the librarian by placing his front paws up on her high desk, so that when she turned around to help this "customer" she nearly fainted and her wig was knocked askew, revealing some rather prominent bald spots. Even the vast lobby of the town's Goldmoor Hotel provides no shelter, for as Emily notes, the "old duffers" who sit there all day spitting tobacco juice into cuspidors cannot stand to see anyone reading, assuming the unfortunate reader must be as bored as they are. In Twainian vernacular Emily speculates on what they must be thinking: " 'I declare, here's somebody worse off than I am. The poor soul's really hard up to have to depend on a book, and it's my bounden Christian duty to help him pass the time,' and they start talking to you. If you want company on the streetcar or the bus . . . open a book and you're all set" (*CS*, 325). The old duffers patronize Emily unmercifully—"laughing and teasing me as if I were a monkey that had suddenly entered their precincts" (*CS*, 325)—recalling Dr. Johnson's famous comment about lady preachers. Finally rejecting the train depot, the Catholic church (since she is a United Presbyterian), and the women's smoking room of the library, Emily settles on the waiting room of the jail, since there are rarely any visitors—or any prisoners, for that matter.

Trying to carve out a space for herself in the distinctly anti-intellectual surroundings of Adams, Emily finds a surprising ally in the town sheriff, Mr. Starbird, who is himself a reader of Fu Manchu mysteries and whose flighty daughters, Ida and Laverne, care for nothing "except what's got on pants" (*CS*, 327). But some rowdy moonshiners are arrested, and the sheriff thinks it best for Emily to leave this rough male environment unsuitable for an innocent young girl. As she wanders toward the trailer camp on the outskirts of town, Emily meets two characters reminiscent of Twain's shiftless, defrauding Duke and King and the inimical Lottie Jump—the evangelist Gerlash and his daughter Opal.

Throughout her descriptions of Adams's gallery of characters, Stafford calls into question Emily's judgment of the town as boring and suggests that the adventure she seeks in books might just as easily be found here. Significantly, Emily is just beginning Twain's *Tom Sawyer Abroad*, an 1894 work narrated by Huck about his travels with Tom and Jim to Egypt and Palestine. A picaresque account of an imaginary journey that borrows heavily from Jules Verne and Sir Walter Scott, Twain's work relies on the humorous dialogue and cultural naïveté of its characters for effect—a situation similar to the one Emily finds herself in with the unscrupulous Reverend and his daughter. But perhaps more importantly, the American edition of *Tom Sawyer Abroad*, which Emily was no doubt reading, had been prudishly expurgated by Mrs. Mabel Mapes Dodge before its serialization in *St. Nicholas Magazine*.[56] A Twain aficionado like Jean Stafford might well have been aware of this fact and used it to ironic advantage in "A Reading Problem." The irony, of course, is twofold: not only has her environment been censored for her by well-meaning guardians of public morality like the sheriff, but the book Emily reads for adventure has also been sanitized, while real adventure awaits her in the unexpurgated pair she meets in Adams's trailer camp.

As in "Bad Characters" and "The Healthiest Girl in Town," Stafford's humor results from clashes of diction: the Reverend's falsely inflated religious rhetoric undercut by Emily's colloquial narrative voice and Opal's straightforward western slang. When the Reverend exhorts Emily to "keep to this path your youthful feet . . . and shun the Sodoms *and* the Gomorrahs," she wryly counters, "My youthful feet were so wet I was having a struggle to put on my socks" (*CS*, 330). When Gerlash mournfully exclaims, "We have had a weary journey, sister," Opal replies with a huge yawn, "You said a mouthful" (*CS*, 331). As the narrative progresses, the Gerlash story unfolds in indirect discourse within the frame device of Emily's own story, further reinforcing the linguistic disparity between the primly bourgeois Emily, who memorizes books of the Bible to get a prize at Sunday school, and the conniving Gerlashes, who similarly spout Bible verses for their nefarious purposes. In fact, the Reverend doesn't even need a Bible, because he has his own 112-page book, titled *Gerlash on the Bible*, which answers such useful questions as "Can Wall Street run God's Business?" (*CS*, 337).

Just as the Gerlashes are about to persuade Emily to go into town and buy them some groceries, Emily's tamed-down surroundings force her to stop short of a real adventure. The sheriff drives up with a deputy and arrests the pair, making Emily a hero for "catching" them. She rides home triumphantly in a police car, clutching her Bible and *Tom Sawyer Abroad*, the putative heroine of her own text. Unfortunately, her fame has spread, and the jail where she is now free to read is full of "copycats" who have decided it makes a good library. Rescued from a real adventure, deprived of space to read (the sheriff is afraid to give her a cell because he doesn't want to ruin her reputation), Emily ends up in the cemetery side by side with another story, "under a shady tree, sitting beside the grave of an infant kinswoman of the sheriff, a late-nineteenth-century baby called Primrose Starbird" (*CS*, 344).

Ten years earlier Jean Stafford had envisioned a tragic fate for Emily's forerunner Molly in *The Mountain Lion*. Molly too has a private space to read, up in a mountain glade, but this glade is violated at the end of the book when her brother Ralph mistakenly shoots her as he hunts the golden mountain lion. Perhaps the leavening distance of time and the comic tone of the Emily Vanderpool stories allowed Stafford to avoid the painful resolution of her earlier novel.

The last of the Emily Vanderpool stories, "The Scarlet Letter," was rejected by Katharine White in her last days as fiction editor of the *New Yorker* and subsequently appeared in *Mademoiselle* in 1959.[57] Typical of Katharine White's encouraging rejections, her note to Stafford praises the earlier Vanderpool stories and their comic narrator, while reluctantly admitting that this one falls short of Stafford's earlier standard. Written during a period when Stafford was turning increasingly to other genres such as film criticism and book reviews, "The Scarlet Letter" is not the equal of its predecessors "Bad Characters" or "A Reading Problem." As in the earlier stories, Emily's comic voice narrates, but the situation she relates is a minor childish prank she and her friend Virgil play on their unsuspecting geography teacher. The prank backfires, and Emily ends up taking the blame when Virgil loses his nerve. They reconcile, with Emily forcing Virgil to vow eternal loyalty: "I ruled him with an iron glove and after he had made one slip he never made another" ("Letter," 101). With the appearance of "The Scarlet Letter," Stafford seems to have mined the comic vein of her childhood material and exhausted the narrative possibilities of Emily Vanderpool.

Beyond Childhood: Another View of the West

The lighthearted tone of Jean Stafford's childhood tales set in the West is notably absent from her western stories with older protagonists. The young women in "The Liberation" (1953), "The Mountain Day" (1956), "The Tea Time of Stouthearted Ladies" (1964), and "The Philosophy Lesson" (1968); the elderly sisters of "In the Zoo" (1955);

Stafford's fictional portraits of her parents and grandparents in her last published story, "Woden's Day" (1979)—all face a world that thwarts and inhibits them, a world without childhood dreams of power and invulnerability. In these stories Stafford treats familiar themes of displacement, isolation, social inferiority, and cultural conflicts between East and West within the larger framework of identity and self-authentication. She explores the inevitable loss of illusion these older characters suffer, often treating thinly disguised autobiographical material from a typically ironic, detached third-person point of view. In most, Adams is clearly delineated in various guises—as the stultifying hometown of Polly Bay in "The Liberation" or of Kitty Winstanley in "The Tea Time of Stouthearted Ladies" or as the locus of childhood misery for Daisy and her sister in "In the Zoo." Like her first published short story, "And Lots of Solid Color," these stories end with characters accepting a life of compromise, accommodation, or at best, dreams of escape.

"The Liberation," appearing in the *New Yorker* in 1953, is the story of Polly Bay, a 30-year-old unmarried woman living with her aunt and uncle in the Bay ancestral home in Adams.[58] Ironically, the trappings of this family mansion are exactly those the young Stafford yearned for—gilt family portraits, brass jardinieres, and tea tables—but Polly finds them stifling as she looks forward to the day when she will leave the house forever to go East and marry her Boston fiancé. She is trapped, however, by a family history that allows her no room for individuality, and by two querulous old relatives whose nagging complaints instill only guilt and fear. Their own children having wisely gone East, Aunt Jane and Uncle Francis "had a vehement family and regional pride, and they counted it virtue in themselves that they had never been east of the Mississippi" (*CS*, 305). Polly finally reveals her plans to them, amid their accusations of disloyalty and lack of family pride. Shortly after this long, painful scene, Polly's sister calls from Boston with the news that her fiancé has died of a heart disease. Stricken but undeterred, Polly boards the last train to Denver on her way to Boston, confident a new life awaits her.

Polly's intended journey ironically reverses the normal westward migration endemic to the frontier myth. Her Bay ancestors had indeed made the journey west across the plains, settling in Adams; had built intimidating stone mansions to house their children and other possessions; and had inevitably been abandoned by these same "heartless" children. Stafford clearly links interior space to psychological space in her descriptions of the vast but crowded rooms of the Bay family mansion: "Its rooms were huge, but since they were gorged with furniture and with garnishments and clumps and hoards of artifacts of Bays, you had no sense of space in them and . . . felt cornered and nudged and threatened by hanging lamps with dangerous dependencies and by the dark, bucolic pictures of Polly's forebears" (*CS*, 308). Stafford's text ultimately subverts the frontier myth of freedom and expansion, for within the wide-open spaces of its rugged mountain environs, Adams offers only imprisonment for women like Polly Bay.

But the vast, looming Bay house symbolizes more than the material wealth the family has accumulated. To Polly it represents an oppressive family history reaching back generations—a text she did not write and from which, she fears, there is no escape. As she bitterly notes, "Nothing can more totally subdue the passions than familial piety" (*CS*, 310). Polly's aunt and uncle are remnants of a once glorious past, a past they will not relinquish but instead relive through their collection of family memorabilia: "cracked photographs, letters sallow-inked with age, flaccid and furry newspaper clippings, souvenir spoons flecked with venomous green, little white boxes holding petrified morsels of wedding cake" (*CS*, 311). In this Dickensian environment Polly realizes with stunning clarity that "she had never once insisted on her own identity in this house" (*CS*, 310). Wistfully, she thinks of her fiancé's stately house in Boston, "at the foot of Beacon Hill, its garden fac[ing] the Charles" (*CS*, 316). It would appear that Polly intends to exchange one house for another, moving from the house of her nouveau riche western relatives to the house of her intended husband. If so, the liberation she so fervently desires may in fact remain beyond her reach, as Aunt Jane's spiteful comment midway through the story suggests. To Polly's impassioned plea "I want to live my own life," she responds, "Being married is hardly living one's own life" (*CS*, 317).

Near the end of the story, as a result of her impassioned declaration of independence, Polly looks at this familiar landscape differently: the mountains seem majestic, and she envisions a time in the future when young Bays will return to the West, "free at last to admire the landscape" without "a trace of the dust of the prairies" (*CS*, 319). She has ultimately invested her surroundings with a sense of her newfound freedom. She leaves for Boston without the hope of an impending marriage, but with the hope of liberation.

Jean Stafford's next story of a young heroine out West was "The Mountain Day," which appeared in the *New Yorker* in 1956.[59] Though

47

not one of her strongest stories, it is instructive for students of Stafford's short fiction because it shows the imprint of Katharine White from its inception. The idea for "The Mountain Day" in fact originated with a story Katharine White told Stafford over lunch, concerning a true incident from White's childhood about two Irish maids who worked for her family in New Hampshire. The maids had gone swimming, stayed out beyond their expected time of return, and were subsequently discovered drowned. The event haunted White for years, and she had even intended to write a story about it herself. Hoping to help Stafford over her writer's block, White shared the material with her, and the result was this story, in which Stafford uses the tragic event as a formative experience in the life of a young woman.

Stafford makes her protagonist a wealthy young eastern woman on holiday out West, where she meets and becomes engaged to a Harvard student doing research at the nearby Science Lodge. One Sunday near the end of summer, they go on an outing, learn of the maids' disappearance, and shortly after find their bodies ravaged by sea turtles. This harrowing experience breaks the young lovers' complacent, secure mood and forces the starry-eyed Judith to move beyond her adolescent fixation on self.

"The Mountain Day," like several of Stafford's other stories, deals with the maturation of a young woman and her burgeoning consciousness of the larger world she is a part of. But on a deeper level, it also dramatizes the seductions and dangers of innocence, not only for Judy, whose Edenic dreams of invulnerability are shattered at the sight of two young maids very much like herself, but also for the Irish maids, whose innocence of their environment ultimately causes their death. Judy's Boston grandmother spends her summer in Colorado, always bringing her maids. This summer it is two "red-haired Irish girls, Mary and Eileen [who] . . . looked down their pretty noses at Mother's servants—local mountain girls who wore ankle socks and cardigans when they served dinner" (*CS*, 240). No doubt lulled into a false sense of security by their mistress's house, which is log cabin outside but pure Boston sitting room inside, the transplanted maids do not believe in the dangers of their rustic environment; consequently, they are not prepared for the sudden mountain storm that capsizes their canoe. At the end of the story, Judy's grandmother, horrified by the incident, vows never to "come here again with innocents" (*CS*, 248). Forced to confront her own naïvéte and self-absorption in the face of someone else's tragedy, Judy also realizes that neither wealth nor family position can finally shield her from the unexpected.

Almost 10 years later, in 1964, Jean Stafford wrote another Adams story, "The Tea Time of Stouthearted Ladies." By the 1960s Stafford was finding it more and more difficult to write fiction, and her projected autobiographical novel *The Parliament of Women* continued to elude her. Whether because of a happy but artistically unproductive marriage to her third husband, journalist A. J. Liebling, or her need for the money journalistic pieces brought, Stafford turned increasingly to other forms of writing during the last two decades of her life. Nevertheless, memories of her childhood and adolescence continued to haunt her, as this 1964 story shows.

Intended to be a part of her unpublished novel *In the Snowfall*, about her college years, "The Tea Time of Stouthearted Ladies" humorously treats one of Stafford's painful memories through its comically ironic tone.[60] The stouthearted ladies of the title are the deluded mothers of hardworking students like Kitty Winstanley—mothers who, like Stafford's own, run boardinghouses for the wealthy college students in Adams. Their husbands pitiful and out of work because of the Great Depression, these women resolutely refuse to face reality. Their kitchen table conversation—a parodic version of a Boston tea—concerns not the exhausting lives of their own children but the lives and loves of their wealthy boarders, who provide them with the vicarious excitement they lack. They romanticize their children's summer jobs, thereby exonerating themselves of guilt as they try to believe their children are leading the good life.

To reinforce this discrepancy between fact and fiction, Stafford's story alternates between two simultaneous narratives: the idealistic musing of Kitty's mother and the other landladies juxtaposed with Kitty's own realistic versions of how she spends her summer vacation: "A little work never hurt anyone, the landladies assured each other, and if it was not Mrs. Winstanley yearning to trade places with Kitty in the debonair life she led as waitress and chambermaid at the Caribou Ranch, it was Mrs. Ewing, similarly self-hypnotized, enumerating the advantages that accrued to her asthmatic son in nightly setting up pins in a bowling alley" (*CS*, 224). The lovely, cool lake Kitty's mother imagines her swimming in is actually icy and full of mud puppies; the sleek horses available for the summer workers are "one spooked and spavined old cow pony the kitchen help could ride"; the lively town of Caribou is really only "a handful of backward people liv[ing] in battered cabins in the shadows of the ore dumps" (*CS*, 225–26). Even the Swiss boarding school–educated Mrs. Bell and Miss Skeen, who own the ranch, though presumed by Kitty's mother to be cultured and selective in their boarders, are secret alcoholics whose nonalcoholic rules force the dudes to buy bootleg liquor. Their hypocrisy, in turn, gives Kitty another source of income, for as we learn near the end of the story, she is their go-between with the bootlegger: "Kitty kept her trysts with Ratty (his eyes were feral and his twitching nose was criminal) and gave him handfuls of money and orders for bottles of atrocious brown booze and demijohns of Dago Red. . . . Kitty had no taste for this assignment of hers—she was not an adventurous girl—but she was generously tipped by the dudes for running their shady errands and for that reason she put up with the risks of it—being fired, being caught by the revenue officers and charged with collusion" (*CS*, 230).

Stafford herself had worked at a dude ranch and at her mother's boardinghouse during the Great Depression—experiences that she kept trying to dramatize in her unpublished novel manuscripts *In the Snowfall* and *The Parliament of Women*, and that she later documents in her 1960 article "Souvenirs of Survival."[61] "The Tea Time of Stout-hearted Ladies" finally brings to light these painful memories of her mother—whom she rarely treated in fiction—and herself as a socially inferior, brainy girl from the West. Notably lacking from this story is any real compassion for the equally victimized mothers, who are forced to live in a dream world merely to survive. In a moment of self-revelation early in the story, Kitty reflects on her pathetic, out-of-work father and her alternately despondent and cheerful mother, but most of all she realizes "she hated herself for hating in them what they could not help" (*CS*, 222). The coldness Kitty feels toward these similarly helpless victims who happen to be her parents might be explained by a comment Stafford made in a 1959 lecture at the University of North Carolina Arts Festival. In it she deplores writing whose purpose is to purge the writer of some past guilt and maintains that "if you write of yourself, you should write with compassion and lay the blame for setting the house on fire on somebody else."[62] This ironic distance came to be a hallmark of Jean Stafford's writing—a literary as well as a psychological device that would characterize her best fiction.

Another Adams story dealing with the events of Stafford's college years was "The Philosophy Lesson," appearing in the *New Yorker* in 1968.[63] (This and the 1979 "An Influx of Poets" would be the last two Stafford stories in the *New Yorker*.) This time the painful memory concerned the suicide of a close friend, Lucy McKee Cooke—an event that haunted Stafford by her own admission and consistently eluded her attempts to give it fictional form. As Carolyn Ezell Foster notes in the introduction to her recently edited portion of Stafford's *In the Snowfall,* "The Philosophy Lesson" was transcribed almost word for word from one of Stafford's many versions of the unpublished manuscript.[64] Its pervasive image of snow would be a familiar one in Stafford's work, both a physical reality from her childhood and a symbol of the peace and detachment she so desired.

The story's protagonist, Cora Savage, poses nude for art classes at the university to make extra money. During one of these sessions, a student bursts in with the news of another student's—Bernard Allen's—suicide. As Cora reflects on this tragic news, she remembers Bernard as "rich, privileged, in love," and the least likely person to commit such a drastic act (*CS*, 369). Cora had, in fact, admired him from afar—envying his social graces, his inexhaustible supply of money, and his beautiful red-haired girlfriend. Jolted out of her idealized dreams of an obviously troubled young man, Cora contemplates the falling snow outside the studio and sees in it a silent blessing for herself and all these "fledgling artists [who] put their own faces on their canvases" (*CS*, 369).

This epiphanic conclusion, so typical of Stafford's short fiction, has, as William Leary points out, a complex of meanings—all relating back to the title and indicating what a conscious literary artist Jean Stafford always was.[65] Earlier in the story Cora remembers a recent philosophy lecture in which the professor had sarcastically referred to Berkeleian idealism as nonsense. Cora, in contrast, welcomed the bishop's theories that material objects have no independent being but exist only as concepts of a human or divine mind, reveling in the notion "that she existed only for herself and possibly for a superior intelligence and that no one existed for her save when he was tangibly present" (*CS*, 365). What she desires, obviously, is a disembodied life—without memory, without unsettling intrusions such as a friend's suicide or the dehumanizing need to make herself into an object for amateur art students. As the story moves toward its conclusion, Stafford alternates Cora's interior monologue with accounts of the art students' responses to Bernard's death. Detached and isolated from them as she always is, Cora believes only she can understand the desolation that must have driven this seemingly sheltered student to take his own life. As Leary notes, she vacillates "between the claims of common humanity and isolating solipsism" (396). The ultimate philosophy lesson for Cora at the story's end is that not only she but "each mortal in the room must, momentarily, have died." They all "had perished in their own particular ways" (*CS*, 369). Like Pansy Vanneman in "The Interior Castle," Cora is inevitably brought back into the material world, whose harsh contours are mercifully blanketed by the pure, white snow.

The most brilliant example of Jean Stafford's Adams stories with older protagonists is the story that received the O. Henry Prize, "In the Zoo" (1955).[66] Charlotte Goodman points out that this story was written during a creative burst of energy in Stafford's career right after her first two volumes of short stories were published in 1953: *Children Are Bored on Sunday* and *The Interior Castle* (Goodman, 237). Narrated by what Goodman calls an older version of Polly Bay in "The Liberation" (240), "In the Zoo" begins with two elderly sisters sitting in a Denver zoo, where they have met to see each other off, as they do after their periodic visits. The blind polar bear they are watching reminds them of Mr. Murphy, a childhood friend. Thus begins a reminiscence of their lonely childhood as orphans raised by a mean-spirited, unloving foster mother, Mrs. Placer, in Adams, Colorado. They remember listening to Mrs. Placer and her boarders complaining about their miserable lives; they remember the dog Mr. Murphy gave them and how Mrs. Placer took him over and trained him to be mean and spiteful like herself; they remember the dog killing Mr. Murphy's monkey, after which Murphy poisoned the dog. Thereafter, Murphy gets older and sicker, and the girls are forbidden to see him. They grow up, their foster mother dies, and both sisters go their own way— one, Daisy, marries and has two sons; the other, the narrator, never marries, and as the story progresses, her strident, whining tone begins to sound more and more like the embittered Mrs. Placer she can never forget.

This story uses a frame technique, literally beginning and ending "in the zoo," enclosing the past in what appears to be an equally grim present. This frame narrative also begins with the narrator ironically describing the zoo animals in distinctly human terms: she imagines that their little community here in the zoo is riddled with all the cruel social snobberies plaguing their human counterparts. Across from the blind polar bear is a cage of "conceited monkeys" who scornfully note his behavior and that of his neighbors, the "stupid, bourgeois grizzlies" (*CS*, 283–84). As they remark on the polar bear's resemblance to Mr. Murphy, a flood of memories returns, bringing with it images of the western town that haunts them: "[W]e are seeing, under the white sun at its pitiless meridian, the streets of that ugly town, its parks and trees and bridges, the bandstand in its dreary park, . . . its mongrel and multitudinous churches, its high school shaped like a loaf of bread, the campus of its college, an oasis of which we had no experience except to walk through it now and then, eyeing the woodbine on the impressive buildings" (*CS*, 285).

Living in the shadow of this Dickensian stepmother who constantly reminds them of her sacrifices and who delights in finding examples of her "solitary creed" that "life was essentially a matter of being done in, let down, and swindled" (*CS*, 286), Daisy and her sister grow up lonely, isolated, and sensitive to the slightest wrongs done to them. In their childhood desperation the sisters find some escape in a precursor of the zoo where the adult sisters find themselves: Mr. Murphy's menagerie of a fox, a skunk, a parrot, a coyote, and two capuchin monkeys whose soulful glances recall a nearly human sorrow. But the focus of all their childhood affections is the puppy Mr. Murphy gives them.

In relentless detail Stafford documents how the embittered "Gran" as Mrs. Placer has them call her, transforms this lovable, harmless animal into a growling, suspicious beast: "Laddy" becomes "Caesar," a tyrant and bully of the weak, and an apt symbol of how Gran poisons everything within her grasp. When Caesar kills Mr. Murphy's monkey, Murphy vows revenge, and the very next day poisons the dog. This grotesque scenario forms the climax of the inner narrative—reinforcing, as Daisy's sister narrates from the perspective of maturity, the sisters' utter powerlessness in the face of such unremitting cruelty. With this example of animalistic behavior, it is no surprise that, as the narrator remarks, she and her sister "lived in a mesh of lies and evasions, baffled and mean, like rats in a maze" (*CS*, 300). Dehumanized by their surroundings, thwarted in their efforts to rise above this crippling environment, the sisters often stare at the massive mountains circling the town and covet their aloofness.

As the story moves toward its bitter conclusion, Stafford makes it clear that while the sisters may have separated themselves geographically from their nightmarish childhood, emotionally they are still trapped there—to an extent even they do not realize. As the sisters prepare to leave, the dialogue they exchange with each other replicates in tone and expression Gran's conversations with her boarders. They complain that the train conductors serve widows and spinsters last;

Daisy notices a woman "nab the redcap [her sister] had signaled to" (*CS*, 302); Daisy's sister suspects the porter of having designs on her luggage; and the alfalfa fields she sees from her train she is certain must be full of marijuana. They seem willing to concede that "life [is] essentially a matter of being done in, let down, and swindled" (*CS*, 286). As Ann Hulbert notes, "In the Zoo," unlike the Emily stories, "reversed the Vanderpool plot line of progress toward healthy maturation" (302). Instead, she continues, what Stafford dramatizes is "an insidious destruction of spirit that rendered her characters . . . anxious souls ill equipped to face the world" (Hulbert, 302).

Though most of Jean Stafford's stories set in the West have female protagonists, there are a few in which she chooses to dramatize familiar themes through male characters. Three notable examples, all quite different from each other, are "A Summer Day" (1948), "A Reasonable Facsimile" (1957), and "Woden's Day" (1979). The first is a tale of an orphaned Native American boy who arrives at the orphanage in the midst of an epidemic; the second is a lighthearted tale of a retired college professor who acquires a voraciously ardent disciple; the last, published posthumously, was the intended first chapter of Stafford's projected novel *The Parliament of Women*, dealing with the family history of the Staffords and McKillops.

Published in the same month and year as "The Bleeding Heart," a tale of an orphaned young girl who yearns to be adopted, "A Summer Day" is the story of Jim Littlefield, an orphaned boy who arrives in Oklahoma barefoot on the train from Missouri.[67] A typical Stafford displaced person, Jim's first impression of the desolate Oklahoma site of the Bureau of Indian Services sharply contrasts with the familiar world he has left behind—a world of rainwater shining in washtubs, wisteria-shaded porches, and trees big enough to sit under. His train ride has been similarly disappointing: even the lunch the preacher's wife had packed for him had "a dead ant on one of the peanut butter sandwiches and the Baby Ruth had run all over the knobby apple" (*CS*, 347). As he waits for someone to show up at the station, he thinks back to the alternative lives he could have had if people back in Missouri had adopted him. Finally rescued by personnel from the orphanage, Jim realizes when they arrive that the deserted playground is the result of an epidemic, and that even at the orphanage he will be isolated. The only other orphan Jim meets is an older boy who represents what Jim could become: a bitter, angry adolescent punished for stealing a gun from Mr. Standing-Deer, and harboring dreams of escape. The story ends with Jim falling into an exhausted sleep, too tired to think of escape.

A more interesting psychological study is Stafford's story "A Reasonable Facsimile," set in the Adams, Colorado, of her childhood stories.[68] The main character is a recently widowed, retired philosophy professor, Dr. Bohrmann, who lives in Adams in a modern glass and stone house he has built for his retirement on the prairie. Determined not to waste away in this remote setting, Bohrmann learns Japanese, keeps up a voluminous correspondence, and lives happily with his cat, Grimalkin, and his housekeeper, Mrs. Pritchard. But he begins an ill-fated correspondence with a young man from the East, Henry Medley, whose wit and learning impress Bohrmann and make him wish for the son he never had. When Medley proposes a visit to Bohrmann, the professor is delighted, and he and his housekeeper begin making preparations.

"A Reasonable Facsimile" is a humorous portrait of discipleship and its attendant, sometimes bizarre complexities. Told from a third-person point of view that accommodates witheringly ironic comments about the young Medley, it may have been based partly on Robert Lowell's similar adoration of his mentor Allen Tate and the reputed episode of the young Lowell building a tent and literally camping out in Tate's yard (Walsh, 17–18). Regardless of its biographical links, the story is a comic depiction of a young scholar who at first appears "respectful, responsive, articulate, enthusiastic, astoundingly catholic in his information," but who gradually reveals a hollowness at the core—"so un-self-centered that Dr. Bohrmann began to wonder if he had a self at all" (*BC*, 76). During their two-year correspondence, Bohrmann is annoyed at Medley's "impassioned, uncritical agreement" (*BC*, 68) with every one of his opinions—even the least carefully thought-out; he chides Medley for his high-handed treatment of college students who don't know Aristotle: "What sort of world would it be if we didn't have the Philistines to judge ourselves by? God bless 'em" (*BC*, 68). But the childless professor is also intrigued by the prospect of molding and shaping this young man's mind, making him "a sort of monument to Dr. Bohrmann after [his] bones were laid to rest" (*BC*, 73).

Transplanted to the West from Freiburg via Montreal, the professor is a tubercular émigré like his colleagues at the university in Adams— all fleeing more illustrious universities because of their affliction. The town of Adams, which is at first "dismaying to European eyes that had been accustomed to grandeur on a smaller scale" (*BC*, 58), gradually seduces Bohrmann and his wife to stay. Stafford is uncharacteristically effusive in her descriptions of the western landscape in this story and of the colony of intellectuals who make up the university. To the Bohrmanns "the immaculate air was deliciously inebriating and the sun, in those superlative heavens, fed them with the vibrancy of youth" (*BC*, 59). Despite the fact that their *New York Times* comes four days late, they exult in the beauties of the landscape and in the charm of its inhabitants. It is to Bohrmann's retreat on the prairie that Henry Medley makes his pilgrimage.

Medley, it turns out, is appropriately named—a fact the professor had suspected all along. The only child of a deceased lawyer father and a penniless mother, he learns a mélange of information, arcane trivia, esoteric enthusiasms; he writes "Miltonic epics and Elizabethan songs" (*BC*, 67); he is indefatigably cultured. Like one of the "dramatis personae of an allegorical play" (*BC*, 68)—as Dr. Bohrmann refers to him in a letter—Medley is distinctly flat: "He would discuss his plans, but not his aspirations; he would talk about his ideas on a subject, but not his feelings on it; he would quote from 'Voyage of the "Beagle,'" but would not say that he longed to go on a voyage himself" (*BC*, 76–77).

He is, during the three weeks he occupies Bohrmann's house, "the most sedulous of apes" (*BC*, 81). Imitating the professor's language and actions, appropriating his role as host, the voracious Medley makes Bohrmann feel his very identity is slipping away from him; it is as if "he had attached to his side an unmovable homunculus, who . . . now spoke German with a Breisgau accent and who mimicked his every thought and every gesture" (*BC*, 82). Bohrmann's epiphanic realization comes as he ironically sees in Medley exactly what he had wished—a mirror image of himself—but sadly lacking in any redeeming humanity. At the story's climax, when Medley enters the professor's bedroom wheezing and asthmatic from the cat, Bohrmann almost takes pity on the pathetic young man, but remembering "the sapping tedium of Medley's monologues and interrogations" (*BC*, 85), he instead advises him to leave. Newly grateful for his house, his cat, and his housekeeper, Bohrmann waves goodbye to this "reasonable facsimile" of himself and contemplates playing bridge with Blossom Duveen, "the bursar's blond and bawdy secretary" (*BC*, 56).

The last story by Jean Stafford to appear in print, "Woden's Day" (1979), was extracted from her unfinished autobiographical manuscript *The Parliament of Women* and published posthumously by her editor and friend Robert Giroux.[69] It stands as an appropriate coda to her life's work not only because it documents what Giroux calls "the prehistory of Adams"[70] and fictionalizes a complex family heritage much like Jean's own, but also because it illustrates Stafford's lifelong artistic struggle to distance herself from the materials of her life. In essays written throughout her life, most notably "Truth in Fiction," she articulated an artistic caveat of calculated detachment from autobiography, advising beginning writers "to winnow carefully and to add a good portion of lies, the bigger the better" ("Truth," 4560). In "Woden's Day" she follows her own advice, as William Leary notes in his article "Grafting onto Her Roots," creating what he calls "allegorical truth" in her attempts to isolate formative influences from her Colorado years—but particularly in her attempt to understand the father figure who was to exercise such power over her later life.[71]

The story begins in 1925 as the tale of two families: the Savages and the McKinnons and their two chief representatives, Dan Savage and Maud McKinnon, modeled on Stafford's father and mother. From this point the narrative retraces an almost 50-year period from the 1880s to 1925. The noble and wicked Wests are embodied in the genteel, religious Maud and the rugged, freethinking Dan, both of whom find their separate ways to Adams via Missouri—Maud as a schoolteacher and Dan as an unlikely gold prospector fresh out of Amity College in Iowa with a degree in classics. Like a Russian novel, Stafford's last story is full of characters who have all played a part in an unfolding family saga and whose role in this recursive narrative can be interpreted from the vantage point of mature reflection and by the authority of a brooding third-person voice. Similar to her earlier stories, it mingles slang, colloquialisms, and regional dialect with archaisms and formal diction.

The most compelling narrative emerging from "Woden's Day" is that of Dan Savage, the cowpunching Greek scholar who despite his rustic upbringing is a definite misfit out West. After his older brother enters law school, Dan is left in Missouri to puzzle over what direction he wants his life to take: "Should he be a scholar? Teach Greek at some high-falutin Eastern college? He read Herodotus, Thucydides, . . . Sophocles and Aeschylus. But then, languid in a hammock on an amber day, he'd be seduced by Vergil and he would meditate on vineyards and bees and growing melons under glass in a pastoral, green land like this thrice-blessed Missouri. He'd had his fill of Longhorn beeves and the crude company of drovers" ("Day," 10). Deciding against a teaching career, Dan instead chooses writing—"he would be Vergil rather than Aristotle" ("Day," 12)—and the life of a country gentleman, overseeing the land he inherits from his father while he writes fiction and philosophical essays. In the picture Dan's mother has taken of him when *Century* magazine accepts his first story, he is sitting at his writing table beside an open window, flowering tree in bloom behind him, his fingers poised delicately as he writes. The picture of youthful optimism, Dan nevertheless reveals from the vantage point of the future telltale signs of what awaits him: "It is a portrait of youth in the youth of a year. You read his mortal vulnerability in his lowered eyes (he does not yet wear thick glasses) and in his bent, clean-shaven neck" ("Day," 14).

Cora Savage is 10 years old when they move to Adams—an event for which she only now understands the causes. Her father's sizable stock market loss precipitates the move, after which their lives—and their father's personality—change drastically. Stafford describes the gradual transformation of an intellectually alive, astute young man into a bitter, defeated misanthrope whose eccentricities embarrass his wife and children and whose demeanor alternates between hurling curses at an unappreciative world and happily whistling arias from *Madame Butterfly*. She remembers his cynical atheism, his tirades against the state and the government, but most of all his sardonic laugh, which seemed to sum up his attitude toward a world he found increasingly alien.

It is hard to speculate where this projected novel would have gone after such a rambling, convoluted first chapter, but reading "Woden's Day" from the perspective of Jean Stafford's other works reveals a text that, though undeniably rooted in a specific time, place, and family history, is on another level a fable of how we all search our past for signs in an attempt to find some redemptive pattern. Before his death on the Wednesday before Thanksgiving, Grandpa McKinnon suffers several strokes—all on Wednesdays, the same day he received postcards from his flighty, runaway daughters vowing they would never come back to Missouri. Thus the title "Woden's Day," which, the learned Dan Savage explains to his children, is the Norse word for Jehovah's Day, a revelation he rounds off with his characteristic laugh. Stafford's text is ultimately a self-reflexive narrative—a pattern of how family histories are constructed: by the slow accretion of fact, fiction, and legend. Its theme is exile, its method a palimpsestic layering of time as Stafford recounts multiple family narratives of leaving home:

daughters, sons, brothers, sisters. At its core is the portrait of the artist as a young man, a sympathetic rendering of an all too human man whose personal and literary heritage Jean Stafford acknowledges in this story. As she says midway through the story in another context: "The pieces were beginning to fit together" ("Days," 21).

Manhattan Island

The last geographic grouping of Jean Stafford's stories, and the last section of her *Collected Stories*, covers her most productive years in the genre of short fiction—1945–56—and contains three of her finest stories: "Children Are Bored on Sunday," "Beatrice Trueblood's Story," and "The End of a Career." Perhaps because Jean Stafford spent so much of her adult life in New York and its environs, all of these stories have female protagonists, from the young girls in "Between the Porch and the Altar" and "Cops and Robbers" to the aging beauty Angelica Early in "The End of a Career."

New York became the scene of triumph and tragedy for Stafford: it would be the site of her Heidelberg homecoming; the setting for some of her young married life with Robert Lowell amid the New York literati; her place of incarceration for alcoholism in Payne-Whitney after her divorce from Lowell; her home with her second and third husbands, Oliver Jensen and A. J. Liebling; the site of her short-lived career as creative writing teacher at Columbia in the 1960s; and finally the place of her death. Though she loved the distractions and diversions of the city throughout her life, Stafford was also dangerously drawn to its anonymity—an experience she dramatizes so poignantly in her first *New Yorker* story, "Children Are Bored on Sunday." From Tenth Street to Fifth Avenue, from the shabby apartment she shared with Lowell to the posh uptown apartment Liebling rented, Stafford traversed New York and its surrounding area geographically and emotionally, sliding up or down the social scale as circumstances dictated. New York ultimately represented the transient existence, the rootlessness, that became the controlling metaphor of her fictional world. As Ann Hulbert notes in her biography of Stafford, New York was "a city of rootless souls among whom [Stafford] saw herself fitting all too well" (263).

The youngest heroine of Stafford's "Manhattan" stories is Hannah of her 1953 *New Yorker* story "Cops and Robbers."[72] Significantly the only story Stafford wrote about a child that was not set in the West, it also lacks the comic edge of these western tales, for it invests the familiar childhood ritual of getting a haircut with emotionally devastating overtones. The seminal event is five-year-old Hannah's trip to the barbershop with her father, where he has her golden curls cut off into a boy's haircut. (The young Stafford had gotten a similar haircut from her father, causing her to go into hiding for days.) But Stafford's narrative focuses not on the incident itself but on its vengeful causes and painful effects in this story of a disintegrating marriage. From the telephone conversation that opens the story, we learn that the night before the trip to the barbershop Hannah's parents had quarreled violently long into the night, resulting in the father's spiteful act.

Throughout the story, Stafford clearly dramatizes what the young Hannah sees as the traumatic consequences of losing the one thing that had not only distinguished her from her siblings but had formed a bond between herself and her mother. Their relationship, the author hints, may be grounded in part on the fact that Hannah's mother sees an image of her own golden beauty in her young daughter: "Actually, her own hair was the same vivacious color and the same gentle texture as Hannah's, and sometimes her hands would leave the child's head and go to her own, to stroke it slowly" (*CS*, 429). Hannah fears the inevitable separation she feels must result from her change in appearance. Further reinforcing Hannah's fear that she won't be loved anymore—"she wondered how long they would keep her now that her sole reason for existence was gone" (*CS*, 428)—is the mother-daughter portrait they had been posing for, which must now be abandoned: " 'It must never be cut,' said the painter one day of Hannah's hair. 'Not a single strand of it' " (*CS*, 430). Hannah's mother becomes the object of her husband's revenge, while Hannah becomes the object of her father's anger and of her family's scorn. She cowers in the stairway at the beginning of the story, listening to her mother relate the painful details of her disfigurement; she cowers in the car, riding home from the barbershop, "hating [her father] bitterly and hating her nakedness" (*CS*, 425). As if a part of herself has been damaged, Hannah's mother is equally insensitive to her daughter's pain. What should have been a humorous family incident turns bitter in this story of a young girl isolated not only from her siblings' games of "cops and robbers" but also from genuine parental affection. Like "The Interior Castle" or "The Philosophy Lesson"—stories that also treat the objectification of women and the terrifying loss of self that ensues—Stafford's "Cops and Robbers" dramatizes a young girl's withdrawal from a world that has become chillingly impersonal, a world in which she feels her identity slipping away. The distant third-person narrative voice of the text reinforces this theme in passages like the following, which combine a child's inarticulate fear with an adult's more detached judgment: "But all the same, no one paid any attention to Hannah; when they spoke of 'the baby,' they might have been speaking of the car or a piece of furniture; one would never have known that she was in the room, for even when they looked directly at her, their eyes seemed to take in something other than Hannah. She felt that she was already shrinking and fading, that all her rights of being seen and listened to and caressed were ebbing away. Chilled and exposed as she was, she was becoming, nonetheless, invisible" (*CS*, 431). This alienation resonates throughout Stafford's story, which, significantly, consists almost entirely of commentary *about* Hannah by her mother and her siblings. Feeling irrevocably isolated from both, Hannah turns to a surrogate mother at the story's end, as she flees to the arms of Mattie, the cook. But after a brief embrace, Mattie too ignores her, leaving Hannah to express her love to the inanimate falling snow, which "fell like sleep" (*CS*, 435) on the branches of the trees.

The young woman in "Between the Porch and the Altar" (1945) experiences a similar sense of loss as she mourns the death of her mother.[73] Though this story is really only an impressionistic vignette, focusing on a young woman's early morning church visit, Stafford chose to include it in her *Collected Stories*; for the student of Stafford's short fiction, it stands as one of the few examples of her fictional treatment of Catholicism and religious faith.[74] Charlotte Goodman speculates that since it was written while Lowell was in a Connecticut prison for draft evasion, the story focuses on the chasm between religious fanaticism and lapsed faith (138). From what he experienced as the flesh-mortifying monasticism of prison, Lowell in fact advised his young wife not to worry about how they would live; God would provide. Indeed, throughout the story the rituals and order of religious belief are contrasted with the chaos and unpredictability of the real world as the unnamed heroine tries unsuccessfully to cloister herself within the sheltering walls of the church while forced to admit the unwelcome intrusions of the material world.

The story reads almost like a fable: the nameless young woman travels through the bitterly cold New York streets to an Ash Wednesday service where secular thoughts overpower her spiritual reflections. Throughout the text, Stafford carefully juxtaposes both dimensions as she depicts a series of all too human encounters on this young woman's quest for religious faith: making her way to church, she meets "a drunken beggar sprawled like a lumpy rug, his feet in ruptured tennis shoes" (*CS*, 408); trying to concentrate on her prayers, she recoils at the sight of black stubble under one of the nuns' coifs; the words of the Gospel ring ironically in her ears—"Lay up to yourselves treasures in heaven . . . where thieves do not break through nor steal" (*CS*, 411); even her intention to light a candle for her friends in China is thwarted by an ugly old crone who asks for her last dime. Reluctantly, she succumbs to this scene of "squalid commerce" at the altar, placing the money in the "clever, metropolitan fingers" of the beggar woman (*CS*, 413).

Through this young woman's eyes, the text unflinchingly examines the externals of the faith and finds them wanting; correspondingly, it reveals the heroine's own spiritual emptiness and inability to see beyond the literal.

Several years later Jean Stafford wrote one of her most brilliant short stories dealing with a crippling retreat from life, "Children Are Bored on Sunday" (1948).[75] Her first *New Yorker* story and the title story of her first collection in 1953, this and her much later "An Influx of Poets" would be her only attempts to fictionalize the literary world she and Robert Lowell had been a part of—and to document its destructive effects on a young woman during that period. Not surprisingly, Stafford's inaugural appearance in the *New Yorker*'s pages was greeted with derision by those very friends, such as John Berryman and Delmore Schwartz, who had attached themselves to the literati she excoriates in her story (Hulbert, 252–60). These poets accused Stafford of slumming among the middlebrow writers and readers of the *New Yorker*. Thus, her dilemma after the story's publication ironically replicated the subtle insults her character Emma experiences at the hands of highbrow New Yorkers on the cocktail party circuit.

Though "Children Are Bored on Sunday" can be compared to actual events, such as Stafford's alienated status among the New York intellectual crowd and her mental breakdown after the divorce from Lowell, the story is perhaps more basically a parable of the lost soul, the marginalized, the outsider, who simultaneously judges herself by the standards of the same world she rejects, and finds in a chance encounter on a Sunday afternoon another similarly wretched soul. Emma and a past acquaintance, Alfred Eisenburg, meet in the Metropolitan museum one cold Sunday by accident. They know each other from the New York social scene, though Emma is not a New Yorker. She thinks of herself as gauche, unsophisticated, and unintellectual. Both she and

Alfred have just been through a nervous collapse—he from divorce and she from some unnamed cause. Their mutual refuge is drink. The story ends with the two of them going to a bar, like two lonely children, to commiserate and "to marry their invalid souls for these few hours of painful communion, . . . to babble with rapture that they were at last, for a little while, no longer alone" (*CS*, 381).

With Emma as its controlling consciousness, "Children . . ." is neatly divided into three distinct sections and moves with grim relentlessness toward its surprisingly lyrical conclusion. Its primary tension emanates from the contrast Emma articulates when she sees Alfred and mentally relives her distance from him and the brittle, intellectual milieu they had once shared. When Emma first catches sight of Alfred as the story begins, she remembers his artificial, stylized world, a place where "cunning guests, on their guard and highly civilized, learnedly disputed on aesthetic and political subjects" (*CS*, 373), seemingly unaware of the encroachments of spring outside the apartment window. Irresistibly awash in memories, Emma resents Alfred's appearance in this, her hiding place, not only because he is an unwelcome reminder of all she does not know about art but also because he conjures up a host of other faces and names from the past. Following a mock-heroic-epic catalog of all the subjects these self-styled specialists pronounce judgments on, the story describes Emma's profound isolation as she is drawn back into Eisenburg's world: "And she saw herself moving, shaky with apprehensions and martinis, and with the belligerence of a child who feels himself laughed at, through the apartments of Alfred Eisenburg's friends, where the shelves were filled with everyone from Aristophanes to Ring Lardner, where the walls were hung with reproductions of Seurat, Titian, Vermeer, and Klee, and where the record cabinets began with Palestrina and ended with Copland" (*CS*, 374).

The first section of Stafford's carefully plotted story ends with a microscopic examination of the cocktail party as drama, a vicious spectacle where hapless souls like Emma are alternately ignored and devoured by the participants, under whose thin veneer of civilization lurks a barely controlled savagery. These parties inevitably degenerate into gossip sessions fueled by alcohol and frequently punctuated by actual physical attacks, which the naive Emma finds it hard to reconcile with the guests' Olympian demeanor. This "species" of partygoer shocks Emma, who believes "urban equal[s] urbane, and ichor r[uns] in these Augustans' veins" (*CS*, 376). From her own Olympian height as detached, ironic judge, Jean Stafford exposes the raw underside of a parasitic social organism.

The story's second section begins with Emma's reflections on the young boys she sees wandering through the museum. Alfred Eisenburg, she decides, would have been one of these "first-generation metropolitan boy[s]" (*CS*, 376), raised in an environment so exotic and alien that Emma can hardly imagine it. Watching the boys examine a suit of armor, Emma thinks back to her arrival in New York at the age of 20, when she is shocked to learn that not everyone had grown up reading Charles Dickens, as she had. These resolute urban intellectuals, in fact, grew up reading Pound's *Cantos*, playing hide-and-seek "behind ash cans" instead of "lilac bushes." One of them "had not heard a cat purr until he was twenty-five" (*CS*, 376). Emma, on the other hand, guiltily believes that "[h]er own childhood, rich as it seemed to her on reflection, had not equipped her to read, or to see, or to listen, as theirs had done; she envied them and despised them at the same time, and at the same time she feared and admired them" (*CS*, 376).

Clearly, Stafford is isolating two modes of relating to the world—the experiential and the intellectual—neither complete in itself. Emma's response to the masterpieces she views on the museum walls is sentient and aesthetic rather than intellectual: she is drawn to the horse's "human and compassionate eyes" in Botticelli's *The Three Miracles of Zenobius*; she admires the peaches in the background of a Crivelli Madonna; Goya's "little red boy inspires in her only the pressing desire to go out immediately in search of a plump cat to stroke" (*CS*, 378).[76] But Emma's education has made it difficult for her to play the genuine intellectual naïf as others had done; instead, she must, college degree in hand, assume a false persona ill-suited to her real self. "Neither staunchly primitive nor confidently *au courant*," Stafford notes, "[Emma] rarely knew where she was at" (*CS*, 378). This section ends with a passage William Leary sees as "an unusual revelation of [Stafford's] bedrock philosophical position" (1987b, 5): "Thus she continued secretly to believe (but *never* to confess) that the apple Eve had eaten tasted exactly like those she had eaten when she was a child . . . and that Newton's observation was no news in spite of all the hue and cry. Half the apples she had eaten had fallen out of the tree, whose branches she had shaken for this very purpose, and the Apple Experience included both the descent of the fruit and the consumption of it, and Eve and Newton and Emma understood one another perfectly in this particular of reality" (*CS*, 379).

Reduced to the same level of suffering humanity by the story's third section, Emma and Alfred finally meet as they leave the museum. Dropping all pretense, they greet each other as long-lost friends, children again, temporarily free to spend a winter Sunday together in New York away from the "grownups." Instantly *"en rapport,"* they understand their mutual addiction to alcohol as they wander off to a bar on Lexington Avenue where "the peace pipe" awaits them (*CS*, 383). The lyrical conclusion of Stafford's story subverts the reader's expectation of a bleak ending. Invoking the image of a heart carved on a tree with the names Emma and Alfred inside, Stafford unites these two lonely souls in an illusory romantic moment in which "all the flowery springtime love affairs that ever were seemed waiting for them in the whisky bottle" (*CS*, 383). In perversely romantic language Stafford ends this story with an image of rebirth, imagining the outcome of Emma and Alfred's meeting as a child, a "separate entity" spawned from this union of two lovers. Leaving the museum, they "scrambled hastily toward this profound and pastoral experience" (*CS*, 383). But perhaps it is no accident that the last picture Emma sees is a Van Eyck diptych of the Judgment Day and the souls in Hell.

Twilight in the City: Jean Stafford's Aging Heroines

The plight of the woman alone was a consistent focus of Jean Stafford's fiction, as the next two stories show. Married three times but living alone for long periods of her life, Stafford was perhaps inordinately attuned to the pleasures and dangers of solipsism—a necessary condition for the writer but not without its social and emotional costs. Characters like Mrs. Chester Ramsey, the general's widow in "The Captain's Gift," and the spinster Jenny Peck in "I Love Someone" are aloof and withdrawn from the larger world, much like Katherine Congreve in Stafford's last novel, *The Catherine Wheel* (1952). They are older versions of Pansy Vanneman in "The Interior Castle," listening from their isolated and silent rooms to the sounds of children playing and friends calling to friends. The impersonal urban landscape serves as a fitting backdrop for these stories of strategic retreat from life.

Secluded in her New York townhouse, Mrs. Chester Ramsey in "The Captain's Gift" (1946)[77] is "an innocent child of seventy-five"

(*CS*, 440), for whom the outside world has grown increasingly unreal. Seemingly oblivious to the passing of time, she lives in one of the few private houses left in her decaying inner-city neighborhood, ensconced amid Victorian antiques and family portraits, imagining the days when she walked among "French nursemaids," "English prams," and "little girls in sailor hats" (*CS*, 438). She masks the unpleasant food smells from the street with "potpourri" and "lemon oil," judging the increasingly ethnic population outside her apartment window crude and animalistic. But the world fails to see Mrs. Ramsey too: on the days when she sits outside dressed in clothes distinctly of another generation, the crowds pass her by as though she were "invisible" (*CS*, 438). Blissfully untouched by sorrow and loss, Mrs. Ramsey elicits no harsh responses from the world, because among its clearly delineated sights and smells she has become a nonentity. Unaware that she has become a bland anachronism, she retreats from the shabby, teeming streets into her placid environment, proclaiming, "I have never liked change, and now I am too old for it" (*CS*, 439).

But the world has indeed changed, as the story makes clear from its first sentence: "Though it is wartime, it is spring, so there are boys down in the street playing catch" (*CS*, 437). Though many of the young men who once came to tea at Mrs. Ramsey's have since left for overseas, though she dutifully copies their military titles and serial numbers clearly onto the letters she writes, though her daughter is a Red Cross supervisor and her son is a military attaché, she projects a stubborn unwillingness to acknowledge this dark side of humanity so jarringly out of place in her calm, harmonious surroundings. The most incongruous note in this unreal world Mrs. Ramsey inhabits is the fact that her deceased husband was a heavily decorated general whose final portrait depicts a man as "keen-eyed" and "imposing" as his wife is cloudy and insubstantial (*CS*, 440).

Retreating into a twilight world of buried consciousness, the general's widow is clearly ill-equipped to face the startling conclusion of the story. Thinking back on her favorite grandson's childhood, Mrs. Ramsey vividly remembers his eager, shining face beside her at concerts, his angelic demeanor as an altar boy at church services. Now a soldier, he has continued to correspond with her, sending presents from around the world and vowing they will ride through Central Park in a carriage when he returns. In a chillingly premonitory statement, he trusts that "he will find her exactly the same as she was when he told her goodbye" (*CS*, 444).

What the young Captain Cousins and his grandmother could not have predicted is the profound change he would undergo as he travels from one arena of war to the other—England, France, Italy, and finally Germany. A growing chill invades the aging townhouse as Mrs. Ramsey opens the present, ironically hoping it will be something unexpected. Out of the tissue paper falls a "braid of golden hair" that once adorned a beautiful girl—"cut off cleanly at the nape of the neck" (*CS*, 445). Its exact source unknown, this brutal reminder of a war whose atrocities were only too real seems to have a life of its own as Mrs. Ramsey tries to imagine the girl who, Stafford grimly interposes, "is hidden from [her] just as Mrs. Ramsey is hidden from the people in the square" (*CS*, 445). In one of the few sentences Mrs. Ramsey utters in this story composed largely of description and retrospective narration, she addresses her absent grandson in words she might have used to chide one who has overstepped the bounds of good manners: "How unfriendly, Arthur!" she says. "How unkind!" But the answering voice she hears resonates with unwanted, inescapable cruelty: "There's a war on, hadn't you heard?" (*CS*, 445)

Six years later Jean Stafford would write her last and most complex novel, *The Catherine Wheel* (1952), whose heroine, Katherine Congreve, remains similarly trapped in the past. Congreve House is an extension of Mrs. Ramsey's aging brownstone, as Katherine's pronouncement— "Not changing is my only occupation"[78]—echoes the earlier heroine's philosophy of stasis. Both women are eerie projections of Stafford in her later years—painfully detached from the post-1960s world, determinedly railing against everything from deplorably modern children's books to the emerging women's movement. This innate conservatism—both literary and political—manifests itself particularly in her older women characters, who live in a densely textured world of antimacassars, silver tea services, Irish linen napkins, and ornate family portraits. Increasingly, Jean Stafford came to resemble the women she had examined with such cold scrutiny, and she of all people would have appreciated the irony in that.

The same year *The Catherine Wheel* appeared, "I Love Someone" was published in the *Colorado Quarterly*.[79] Like Mrs. Ramsey in "The Captain's Gift," Jenny Peck, a spinster, lives alone, and as the story opens she is mourning the recent suicide of a friend. In a lyrical, meditative first-person voice, Jenny tells her own story of a Jamesian unlived life, rational, ordered, and sterile. She is conscious, at the age of 43, that she has become a character in her friends' myth-making, a spinster by circumstance, not choice. To explain her situation, they invent a lost love for her, killed perhaps in a war, or wasting away in a tuberculosis sanitarium. They could not face the inescapable fact that becomes clear from Jenny's poignant monologue—that she has chosen this solitary life. As she confesses, "From childhood I have unfailingly taken all the detours around passion and dedication; or say it this way, I have been a pilgrim without faith, traveling in an anticipation of loss, certain that the grail will have been spirited away by the time I have reached my journey's end" (*CS*, 418). She wonders if these friends wish she, without husband and children, had been the one to die rather than their beautiful, charming friend Marigold, dead of an overdose of sleeping pills and leaving a husband and two sons behind.

In a haunting visual image Jenny sees scrawled on the sidewalk—a childishly drawn heart with the cryptic legend "I Love Someone"— Stafford locates the mystery of identity that lies at the core of her fictional world. Anonymous, plaintive, unknowable, the childish scrawl reveals neither the lover nor the beloved, Jenny ruefully notes. Instead, it expresses the paradox of an intensely personal sentiment couched in clinically impersonal words, a verbal icon summarizing the imaginary life Jenny's friends have constructed for her and in which she wraps herself like a shroud. In a moment of somber realization, Jenny reflects that she is "more dead now, this evening, than Marigold Trask in her suburban cemetery" (*CS*, 418). Stripped of her true identity by her well-meaning friends, she is willing to accept her friends' diagnosis of spinsterhood as an "incurable but unblemishing disease" (*CS*, 419). To admit the truth to her peers would destroy their illusions.

As Jenny Peck meditates on her friend's suicide, contrasting this irrational act with her own always rational behavior, noise from the courtyard outside intrudes on her reveries: a neighborhood gang of boys is fighting outside her window. Drawn to the brutal spectacle, which contrasts so strongly with the tomblike silence of her apartment, Jenny watches until one of the boys emerges the bloody victor. In a strange moment of naked communication, he glances up at the curious, staring woman and shrugs his shoulders as if to assert the essential rightness of what he has just done. Shaken out of her placid mood, Jenny rushes outside, propelled by some inner necessity to be in touch with a vital world she rarely allows to touch her. Once she is out on the street, her purpose becomes clear: "I realize that I want to see the ruffians face to face, both the undefeated and the overthrown, to see if I can penetrate at last the mysterious energy that animates everyone

69

in the world except myself" (*CS*, 422). But she fails to reach her destination, stopped abruptly by the crudely scrawled heart, which she imagines could easily proclaim its opposite—a message of hate or of love. As a graphic echo of her own indifferent, anonymous life, the bloated heart becomes Jenny Peck's epiphany, a final tragic self-realization: "My friends and I have managed my life with the best of taste and all that is lacking at this banquet where the appointments are so elegant is something to eat"(*CS*, 422).

Jenny Peck is one of many female characters who—single, divorced, widowed—become paradigmatic of the modern condition Jean Stafford so eloquently dissects. Young or old, these women seldom thrive. More often, they retreat into a world of fantasy, as Rose Fabrizio in "The Bleeding Heart"; denial, as Mrs. Ramsey in "The Captain's Gift"; or bitter memories, as the sisters from "In the Zoo." Even marriage rarely fulfills, as powerful stories like "A Country Love Story" and "A Winter's Tale" document. Married women in Stafford's fiction are trapped in loveless unions, driven to create fantasy lovers or doomed to live in a past of bittersweet memories. When the complicating factors of abusive lovers or encroaching old age enter the picture, as in the last two stories of this section—"Beatrice Trueblood's Story" and "The End of a Career"—the situation takes a decidedly somber turn.

Stafford's story "Beatrice Trueblood's Story" appeared in the *New Yorker* in 1955.[80] The plot concerns Beatrice Trueblood, who, two months before her second marriage, suddenly becomes deaf. As the story unravels, we discover that her parents had been locked into a loveless, abusive marriage—her mother's alcoholism aggravated an already shaky union—and that Beatrice's first marriage had likewise been to an abusive alcoholic. The prospects for her second marriage had seemed ideal: Marten ten Brink was a rich, dependable, boring man who seemed a perfect haven for Beatrice. But a family friend, Jack Onslager, during a long Newport weekend overhears a violent quarrel between Beatrice and Marten, after which the deafness strikes. Onslager too had often wished for such a temporary respite from the interminable round of social engagements his wealthy status required, and so he is instantly sympathetic toward and curious about Beatrice's affliction. Sent to urge Bea to see a psychoanalyst, Onslager finds out that, in order to flee her fiancé's jealous rantings, she has willed herself deaf—and has inexplicably been granted her wish.

Stafford's original version of this story bore the title "Patterns," an ominous and ironic choice, as Ann Hulbert notes, for, 20 years after the story was published, Jean Stafford would become a victim of a cruel aphasia that impaired her speech and effectively silenced this once so witty and garrulous raconteur (Hulbert, 306). Though Stafford could scarcely have foreseen this fate, in retrospect it makes "Beatrice Trueblood's Story" strangely resonant.

As a study of a psychosomatic retreat from life amid a brittle East Coast social milieu, Stafford's narrative takes place in an appropriately Whartonian setting, alternating between the lawns of Newport and Bea's sterile New York apartment. As the story begins, Bea's friend Priscilla Onslager is telling the story of Bea's deafness to an assemblage of weekend guests at her Newport home. Ascribing her friend's situation to an untoward "fate," Priscilla proceeds to tell the sad story of Bea's "hideous" childhood, her poverty, her marriage to Tom Trueblood, and the final cruel irony that broke her engagement to the "scrumptiously rich" Marten ten Brink (*CS*, 386). Quick to pass judgment and to assign motives, Priscilla and her audience gossip, speculate, categorize, and otherwise dissect the unhappy woman's life, confident in their smug social superiority that they know her story. When a defrocked clergyman in the group tentatively suggests that Bea broke the engagement because she simply did not want to marry Marten, Priscilla vehemently denies the possibility. Like Jenny Peck's friends in "I Love Someone," Beatrice Trueblood's friends construct a narrative about her that fits their version of the world, unaware that the protagonist of their invented drama has already subverted their careful plotting.

Stafford's own dissection of the Newport social milieu continues with her shift to Jack Onslager, Priscilla's husband, who listens to her long-winded tale and wishes that he, like Beatrice, could just close his ears and "seal himself into an impenetrable silence" (*CS*, 388). As a sympathetic, distanced male character who views his opulent world with scorn and boredom, Onslager provides a crucial narrative voice in Beatrice Trueblood's story, for he alone appears to know the depth of her despair and he alone wishes to share in her dramatic response. As he listens to his wife, Jack has a flashback to his Gatsbyesque life, which seems from his present vantage point like a "colossal *tableau vivant* that would vanish at the wave of a magic golden wand" (*CS*, 389). Admittedly bewitched by the women who glide across the endless ballroom floors, he views their actions and intrigues "with the accuracy of the uninvolved bystander," and ironically reflecting his wife's myth-making urge, he too "devise[s] . . . fiction[s]" about his friends, seduced by what he sees as the drama of their lives (*CS*, 390). But Onslager is considerably more perceptive and intuitive than his peers, and it is he who really knows Beatrice Trueblood's story. Amid the romantic unrealities these shallow socialites luxuriate in, Onslager's harshly realistic text emerges as an ironic corrective.

Onslager's flashback ends with his memory of Beatrice walking serenely down the lawn to cocktails before lunch, unaware of her affliction. Locked in her blessed silence, she gradually realizes she cannot hear the aimless conversation of her friends, and with a look Priscilla and the others take to be terror but Jack knows to be "one of revelation," she announces, "I am deaf. That explains it" (*CS*, 396). As the narrative shifts back to the present and the determined recommendations of Bea's friends that she first see a psychoanalyst and then get a husband, the clergyman articulates the key to Beatrice's behavior in his comments to the sympathetic Jack. It is the power of the will, he believes, that lies behind her predicament—a will that in this case has "cease[d] to be an agent and become a despot" (*CS*, 397).

With this summation the story moves to an urban setting in every way the antithesis of Newport's manicured lawns and billowy white sails. Beatrice's prosaic new apartment building in the East Seventies is "an odious mustardy brown," surrounded by the sights and sounds of the city: obscenity-spouting gangs of angry boys, sprawling bums on the sidewalk, and women leaning out of windows discussing the unbearable heat. Typical of Stafford, the descriptions of the apartment and its surroundings firmly ground her character in a realistic environment that serves to underscore Beatrice's reduced circumstances and, by contrast, Jack Onslager's involuntary snobbery. Assaulted by the dim lighting, green plastic cushions, and wheezing elevator, he cannot help but think how much better off his friend would be ensconced in the opulent surroundings of Marten ten Brink's apartment. As this urban scene develops, Bea confesses the truth of her condition, which Jack already knows, admitting her fear and loneliness and her profound dread of confrontation: "She hated any kind of quarrel, she said . . . but she could better endure a howling brawl among vicious hoodlums, . . . a degrading jangle between servant and mistress, than she could the least altercation between a man and a woman whose conjunction had had as its origin tenderness and a concord of desire" (*CS*, 401).

After her confession, Beatrice tells Jack a considerably muted version of her childhood and previous marriage, all the while reminiscing about the horrifying truth of her parents' ill-fated, destructive relationship—

which began her lifelong desire to escape. Stafford's brilliant use of the omniscient point of view allows us to contrast the two narratives at this turning point in the story, as we mentally juxtapose the "story" Jack is hearing with the reality the author reveals through Bea's reminiscence.

Manuscript versions of this story indicate some confusion in its original version at precisely this point in the narrative. Katharine White's editorial commentary—which Stafford wisely followed—indicates her own confusion as to whether Bea is telling the horrendous truth of her past or merely remembering it. In the revised version Stafford clarifies with the introductory sentence to this section: "As Beatrice talked in discreet and general terms and candidly met Jack Onslager's eyes, in another part of her mind she was looking down the shadowy avenue of all the years of her life" (*CS*, 401).

Another editorial change suggested by White concerns the ending of Stafford's story. In previous versions Stafford had Beatrice marry ten Brink and shortly thereafter die. Instead of this somewhat melodramatic and extreme conclusion, White suggests Bea marry someone else after she regains her hearing, but rather than die, simply live in yet another fated version of her parents' miserable union. This, in fact, is how the story ends: in the last section Bea marries a poor research chemist who, in her friends' deluded eyes, appears to make her deliriously happy. But a conversation Jack Onslager happens to overhear between the newlyweds, coupled with his earlier perceptive observations of them, confirms his suspicions: "He himself had never seen a face so drained of joy, or even of the memory of joy; he had not been able to meet Bea's eyes" (*CS*, 404). In this intimate glimpse of another chapter in Beatrice Trueblood's story, the reader sees a devastating cycle of defeat mirrored in the story's circular plot. Trapped in a text where she seems fated to be eternal victim, Beatrice Trueblood is one of Jean Stafford's memorable women for whom a strategic retreat from life into the interior castle of her mind ultimately proves impossible.

The last story in *Collected Stories*, aptly titled "The End of a Career" (1956), is a narrative of an aging beauty who, like Beatrice Trueblood, becomes a creation of her friends' adoring glances and the vehicle of their desires.[81] But Stafford not only trenchantly satirizes society's expectations of beautiful women; she also, as the story's title suggests, explores the powerful dynamic that exists between a writer and her audience—a subject that, at 41 and in midcareer, she inevitably contemplated.

"The End of a Career" is the story of Angelica Early, whose unearthly beauty makes her an international celebrity and a frequent guest at glamorous dinner parties, where she graces the table like a glittering ornament. Married to an obtuse, rather insensitive big-game hunter whose frequent absences give her considerable freedom to pursue her beautifying rituals, Angelica feels an obligation not only to herself but to her admirers to maintain the beauty that so animates their lives. In an artfully compressed introductory paragraph, Stafford describes Angelica in the words of her adoring public as a "nymph in her cradle" and a "goddess" in her "silvery coffin," thus framing this woman's pathetic life in a few sentences and foreshadowing the story's inevitable conclusion (*CS*, 447).

When her hands begin to show her age, Angelica hides from the world, spreads the rumor that she is dying of cancer, and takes to her bed. Angelica's aunt visits at the end of the story, bringing the languishing invalid a beautiful pair of embroidered gloves. After her initial hysteria Angelica slips the gloves on as she lies in bed. As the story ends, the maid who comes in later in the day finds her dead of a heart attack.

From the beginning of the story, Stafford depicts Angelica as a beautiful object, a passive, shallow woman not rich enough to be interesting to the truly rich, not chic enough to set fashion trends, not intelligent enough to utter any profound observations, not even flirtatious enough to incur the wrath of other women. Childless, without any center to her life except the religious devotion to her face and body, Angelica recalls Edith Wharton's Lily Bart from *The House of Mirth*, a beautiful adornment in her rigidly hierarchical, ultimately fickle world, and like Angelica, a victim of her own innocence. Angelica has no friends, but an "entourage" like a "public personage," though her smitten male admirers quickly discover that very little substance lies under the beautiful facade (*CS*, 450). With nunlike dedication Angelica has withdrawn from life and—like far too many American women, Stafford implies—devoted herself to the religion of the body: "[S]he was consecrated to her vocation and she had been obliged to pass up much of the miscellany of life that irritates but also brings about the evolution of personality; the unmolested oyster creates no pearl" (*CS*, 450–51).

Little do Angelica's admirers suspect the tortuous rituals she undergoes, from applying her makeup in front of mirrors that cast "an image of ruthless veracity" (*CS*, 451) to making yearly trips to a plastic surgeon in France who painfully scrapes her skin to maintain the illusion of youth.[82] These annual trips incite her friends to speculate that the renewed passion they see in Angelica comes from a secret lover who has given her life new purpose. Angelica's "passion" is, of course, herself and the endless attention her now aging face and body require. Significantly, she assumes an alias when she visits the sanitarium, thereby divesting herself of any personal identity and intensifying Stafford's implication that, for women like Angelica, the image *is* the self. Faced with the prospect of aging beyond the control of her masterful plastic surgeon (who advises her to get a lover), Angelica fears the emptiness ahead and regrets not "lay[ing] up a store of good things against the famine of old age" (*CS*, 457).

The adoring public that contributed to Angelica's narcissism also victimizes her. When she overhears a cruel comment about her hands spoken by two young men, Angelica begins her painful downward spiral, withdraws from the world, and finally loses the will to live.

The story's numerous pointed references to art and the artist, beginning with the title, make the analogy clear and add another dimension to this parable of an ill-fated beautiful woman. Like Angelica, the artist labors to construct an illusion—a fiction—requiring constant labor and devotion that are largely invisible to her audience: "The world kindly imagined that Mrs. Early's beauty was deathless and that it lived its charmed life without support" (*CS*, 451). Both beauty and artistic talent imply obligation and incur expectations: a fickle public is quick to see the chinks in the edifice, the flaws in the marble. As Jean Stafford found the writing of fiction increasingly difficult in the last 20 years of her life, as literary fashions inevitably shifted, she might well have voiced the request Angelica poses near the end of the story: "I was faithful to your conception of me for all those years. Now take pity on me—reward me for my singleness of purpose" (*CS*, 460).

Jean Stafford placed "The End of a Career" last in her 1969 *Collected Stories*, thus punctuating her life's work with a story whose obvious subject is woman but whose deeper subtext is writer. Mediating between these two often conflicting identities was never easy for Stafford, though in stories like "The End of a Career" she articulates the tensions and demands of both roles more lucidly than she ever would in life. Studiously avoiding artist figures in her work, Stafford nevertheless wrote, in various guises, a composite portrait of the woman artist—from the childhood adventures of Emily Vanderpool to the wistful meditations of the aging Angelica Early.

Notes to Part 1

1. Mary Ann Wilson, "In Another Country: Jean Stafford's Literary Apprenticeship in Baton Rouge," *Southern Review* 29 (Winter 1993): 58–66.

2. Jean Stafford, "Truth in Fiction," *Library Journal* 91 (October 1966): 4559; hereafter cited in the text as "Truth."

3. Charlotte Goodman, *Jean Stafford: The Savage Heart* (Austin: University of Texas Press, 1990), 187; hereafter cited in the text.

4. Scott Elledge, *E. B. White: A Biography* (New York: W. W. Norton, 1984), 182.

5. Jean Stafford, "On Writing," unpublished lecture delivered at Barnard College, 1971, file A, Lectures and Plays, Jean Stafford Collection, Special Collections Department, University of Colorado at Boulder Libraries.

6. See Linda H. Davis, *Onward and Upward: A Biography of Katharine S. White* (New York: Fromm International, 1987); hereafter cited in the text.

7. Linda Davis's biography of Katharine White documents her maternal, nurturing relationship to other gifted writers, such as May Sarton, S. J. Perelman, and Joseph Mitchell.

8. William Leary's article "Jean Stafford, Katharine White, and the *New Yorker*" (*Sewanee Review* 93 [Fall 1985]: 584–96) also documents the White-Stafford relationship.

9. Jean Stafford, "Don't Use Ms. with Miss Stafford, unless You Mean ms.," *New York Times*, 21 September 1973, 36.

10. Jean Stafford, review of *Les Belles Images*, by Simone de Beauvoir, *Vogue*, 15 March 1968, 46.

11. Jean Stafford, letter to Robert Lowell, n.d., Houghton Library, Harvard University, Cambridge, Massachusetts (quoted in Goodman p. 176).

12. Maureen Ryan, *Innocence and Estrangement in the Fiction of Jean Stafford* (Baton Rouge: Louisiana State University Press, 1987), 9; hereafter cited in the text.

13. See Dana Heller, *The Feminization of Quest-Romance: Radical Departures* (Austin: University of Texas Press, 1990), for her discussion of the primacy of the quest-romance form in Stafford's fiction.

14. Jean Stafford, "The Home Front," *Partisan Review* 12 (Spring 1945): 149–69. Reprinted in Jean Stafford, *Children Are Bored on Sunday* (New York: Harcourt, Brace, 1953), 104–42; hereafter cited in the text as *CABS*.

15. Jean Stafford, "The Maiden," *New Yorker*, 29 July 1950, 21–25. Reprinted in Jean Stafford, *The Collected Stories of Jean Stafford* (New York: Farrar, Straus & Giroux, 1969), 55–64; hereafter cited in the text as *CS*.

16. Marjorie Stafford Pinkham, "Jean," *Antaeus* 52 (Spring 1984): 27.

17. Jean Stafford, "It's Good to Be Back," *Mademoiselle*, July 1952, 26.

18. Jean Stafford, "The Echo and the Nemesis" (originally published as

"The Nemesis"), *New Yorker*, 16 December 1950, 28–35. Reprinted in *CS*, 35–53.

19. Sandra Gilbert and Susan Gubar, *The Madwoman in the Attic: The Woman Writer and the Nineteenth-Century Literary Imagination* (New Haven: Yale University Press, 1979); hereafter cited in the text.

20. Jean Stafford, *A Winter's Tale*, in *New Short Novels* (by Jean Stafford, Elizabeth Etnier, Shelby Foote, and Clyde Miller), vol. 1, ed. Mary Louise Aswell (New York: Ballantine, 1954). Reprinted in Jean Stafford, *Bad Characters* (New York: Farrar, Straus & Giroux, 1964), 225–76; hereafter cited in the text as *BC*.

21. Jean Stafford, "My Blithe, Sad Bird," *New Yorker*, 6 April 1957, 30–38. Reprinted in *Prize Stories 1958: The O. Henry Awards*, ed. Paul Engle (New York: Doubleday, 1958), 79–97; hereafter cited in the text as *PS*.

22. Eileen Simpson, *Poets in Their Youth: A Memoir* (New York: Random House, 1982), 131.

23. Jean Stafford, "The Children's Game" (originally published as "The Reluctant Gambler"), *Saturday Evening Post*, 4 October 1958, 35, 90–92, 94. Reprinted in *CS*, 19–33.

24. Jean Stafford, "Maggie Meriwether's Rich Experience," *New Yorker*, 25 June 1955, 24–30. Reprinted in *CS*, 3–17.

25. Jean Stafford, "Caveat Emptor" (originally published as "The Matchmakers"), *Mademoiselle*, May 1956, 116, 166–73. Reprinted in *CS*, 75–90.

26. Mark Twain, "How to Tell a Story," *Youth's Companion*, 3 October 1895. Reprinted in *Selected Shorter Writings of Mark Twain*, ed. Walter Blair (Boston: Houghton Mifflin, 1962), 239–45.

27. William Leary, "A Tale of Two Titles: Jean Stafford's 'Caveat Emptor,' " *South Atlantic Quarterly* 85 (Spring 1986): 126.

28. Jean Stafford, "The Hope Chest," *Harper's*, January 1947, 62–65. Reprinted in *CS*, 113–19.

29. Jean Stafford, letter to William Mock, 2 December 1939 (quoted in Goodman, 89).

30. Jean Stafford, *Boston Adventure* (Philadelphia: Blakiston, 1944), 247.

31. Jean Stafford, "Polite Conversation," *New Yorker*, 20 August 1949, 24–28. Reprinted in *CS*, 121–32.

32. Jean Stafford, "A Country Love Story," *New Yorker*, 6 May 1950, 26–31. Reprinted in *CS*, 133–45.

33. Susan Rosowski, "The Novel of Awakening," in *The Voyage In: Fictions of Female Development*, ed. Elizabeth Abel, Marianne Hirsch, and Elizabeth Langland (Hanover, N.H.: University Press of New England, 1983), 49; hereafter cited in the text.

34. Jean Stafford, "An Influx of Poets," *New Yorker*, 6 November 1978, 43–60; hereafter cited in the text as "Poets."

35. Jean Stafford, "The Interior Castle," *Partisan Review* 13 (November–December 1946): 519–32. Reprinted in *CS*, 179–93.

36. Jean Stafford, "The Bleeding Heart," *Partisan Review* 15 (September 1948): 974–96. Reprinted in *CS*, 147–70.

37. Jean Stafford, "Life Is No Abyss," *Sewanee Review* 60 (July 1952): 465–87. Reprinted in *CS*, 93–112.

38. Jean Stafford, "New England Winter," *Holiday*, February 1954, 36.

39. Eudora Welty, *Place in Fiction*, quoted in *Storytellers and Their Art*, ed. Georgianne Trask and Charles Burkhart (Garden City, N.Y.: Doubleday, 1963), 253.

40. See Elaine Showalter, "Feminist Criticism in the Wilderness," *Critical Inquiry* 8 (Winter 1981): 202–3.

41. See Susan Armitage, "Western Women's History: A Review Essay," *Frontiers* 5 (Fall 1980): 71–73, and Annette Kolodny, *The Land before Her* (Chapel Hill: University of North Carolina Press, 1984).

42. Jean Stafford, "Enchanted Island," *Mademoiselle*, May 1950, 40.

43. Melody Graulich, "Jean Stafford's Western Childhood: Huck Finn Joins the Camp Fire Girls," *Denver Quarterly* 18 (Spring 1983): 39–55.

44. Jean Stafford, "And Lots of Solid Color," *American Prefaces* 5 (November 1939): 22–25; hereafter cited in the text as "Color."

45. Jean Stafford, "The Darkening Moon," *Harper's Bazaar*, January 1944, 60, 96–98, 100. Reprinted in *CS*, 251–62.

46. Mary Ellen Williams Walsh, "The Young Girl in the West: Disenchantment in Jean Stafford's Short Fiction," in *Women and Western Literature*, ed. Helen Winter Stauffer and Susan J. Rosowski (Troy, N.Y.: Whitston Publishing, 1982), 240; hereafter cited in the text.

47. See also Joanna Russ, *The Heroine's Text* (New York: Columbia University Press, 1980).

48. Alice Dixon Bond, "Fascination with Words Started Jean Stafford on Writing Career" (interview), *Boston Sunday Herald*, 27 January 1952, n.p.; hereafter cited in the text.

49. Jean Stafford, "The Healthiest Girl in Town," *New Yorker*, 7 April 1951, 32–40. Reprinted in *CS*, 197–217.

50. David Roberts, *Jean Stafford: A Biography* (Boston: Little, Brown, 1988), 311; hereafter cited in the text.

51. Howard Moss, "Jean: Some Fragments," *Shenandoah* 30 (Autumn 1979): 79.

52. Jean Stafford, "The Violet Rock," *New Yorker*, 26 April 1952, 35; hereafter cited in the text as "Rock."

53. Jean Stafford, "Plight of the American Language," *Saturday Review World*, 4 December 1973, 18.

54. Jean Stafford, "Bad Characters," *New Yorker*, 4 December 1954, 42–51. Reprinted in *CS*, 263–82.

55. Jean Stafford, "A Reading Problem," *New Yorker*, 30 June 1956, 24–32. Reprinted in *CS*, 323–44.

56. John C. Gerber, *"Tom Sawyer Abroad,"* in *The Mark Twain Encyclopedia*, ed. J. R. LeMaster and James D. Wilson (New York: Garland, 1993), 739.

57. Jean Stafford, "The Scarlet Letter," *Mademoiselle*, July 1959, 62–68, 100–1; hereafter cited in the text as "Letter."

58. Jean Stafford, "The Liberation," *New Yorker*, 30 May 1953, 22–30. Reprinted in *CS*, 305–22.

59. Jean Stafford, "The Mountain Day," *New Yorker*, 18 August 1956, 24–32. Reprinted in *CS*, 231–49.

60. Jean Stafford, "The Tea Time of Stouthearted Ladies," *Kenyon Review* (Winter 1964): 116–28. Reprinted in *CS*, 219–30.

61. Jean Stafford, "Souvenirs of Survival: The Thirties Revisited," *Mademoiselle*, February 1960, 90–91, 174–76.

62. Jean Stafford, "Young Writers," *Analects* 1 (October 1960): 23.

63. Jean Stafford, "The Philosophy Lesson," *New Yorker*, 16 November 1968, 59–63. Reprinted in *CS*, 361–69.

64. Carolyn Ezell Foster, "Introduction to Jean Stafford's *In the Snowfall*," *South Carolina Review* 24 (Spring 1992): 140.

65. William Leary, "The Suicidal Thirties: Jean Stafford's 'The Philosophy Lesson,' " *Southwest Review* 72 (1987): 389–403; hereafter cited in the text as Leary 1987a.

66. Jean Stafford, "In the Zoo," *New Yorker*, 19 September 1953, 24–32. Reprinted in *CS*, 283–303.

67. Jean Stafford, "A Summer Day," *New Yorker*, 11 September 1948, 29–35. Reprinted in *CS*, 345–59.

68. Jean Stafford, "A Reasonable Facsimile," *New Yorker*, 3 August 1957, 20–30. Reprinted in *BC*, 55–87.

69. Jean Stafford, "Woden's Day," *Shenandoah* 30 (Autumn 1979): 10; hereafter cited in the text as "Day."

70. Robert Giroux, "A Note about 'Woden's Day,' " *Shenandoah* 30 (Autumn 1979): 5.

71. William Leary, "Grafting onto Her Roots: Jean Stafford's 'Woden's Day,' " *Western American Literature* 23 (1988): 135. Leary's article documents intentional factual discrepancies in the story.

72. Jean Stafford, "Cops and Robbers" (originally published as "The Shorn Lamb"), *New Yorker*, 24 January 1953, 28–34. Reprinted in *CS*, 423–35.

73. Jean Stafford, "Between the Porch and the Altar," *Harper's*, June 1945, 654–57. Reprinted in *CS*, 407–13.

74. For a more detailed treatment of Catholicism in Jean Stafford's works, see my article "From Romance to Ritual: Jean Stafford, Robert Lowell, and Catholicism," *Xavier Review* 12 (Spring 1992): 36–45.

75. Jean Stafford, "Children Are Bored on Sunday," *New Yorker*, 21 February 1948, 23–26. Reprinted in *CS*, 373–83.

76. William Leary's article "Pictures at an Exhibition: Jean Stafford's 'Children Are Bored on Sunday' " (*Kenyon Review* 49 [Spring 1987]: 1–8) discusses at length the role of painting in Stafford's story; hereafter cited in the text as Leary 1987b.

77. Jean Stafford, "The Captain's Gift" (originally published as "The Present"), *Sewanee Review* 54 (April 1946): 206–15. Reprinted in *CS*, 437–45.

78. Jean Stafford, *The Catherine Wheel* (New York: Harcourt, Brace, 1952), 173.

79. Jean Stafford, "I Love Someone," *Colorado Quarterly* 1 (Summer 1952): 78–85. Reprinted in *CS*, 415–22.

80. Jean Stafford, "Beatrice Trueblood's Story," *New Yorker*, 26 February 1955, 24–32. Reprinted in *CS*, 385–405.

81. Jean Stafford, "The End of a Career," *New Yorker*, 21 January 1956, 35–42. Reprinted in *CS*, 447–63.

82. Jenijoy La Belle's 1988 study, *Herself Beheld: The Literature of the Looking Glass* (Ithaca, N.Y.: Cornell University Press), is a fascinating study of mirrors and female self-definition in literature. Many of her observations are germane to Stafford's "The End of a Career."

Part 2

THE WRITER

Introduction

Though Jean Stafford was the most conscious of literary artists, she made few critical pronouncements about the art of writing fiction. When asked to comment on her writing—its rituals, methods, philosophy—Stafford would sometimes adopt a "Miss McKeehan–like" persona (that of a college professor she admired) and profess the ultimate mystery of the writing process, retreating from a rigid formulation of artistic tenets behind the ironic pose that served her so well in her fiction. Nevertheless, an artistic philosophy does emerge in the following excerpts: from an artist's necessity to remain close to her roots (as in the 1952 "An Etiquette for Writers") to the equally necessary love and knowledge of the language that always animated Stafford's best fiction ("The Felicities of Formal Education").

In "An Etiquette for Writers," Jean Stafford speaks fondly of the western landscape that was such a formative influence on her finely honed sense of place, articulating her own personal dislocation on returning to the West from New England. These comments enrich our reading of not only Stafford's western stories but also those set in regions she subsequently adopted as home. Twenty years later, in "The Felicities of Formal Education," a lecture she delivered at Barnard in 1971, Stafford takes a backward look at her own literary evolution before the days of television, lamenting in her typical tongue-in-cheek mode her narrowly literary knowledge while at the same time berating the contemporary rush toward a "relevant" education. Reading the typescript of this lecture sheds new light on stories like "Caveat Emptor," which satirize progressive education and its attendant problems.

In these selections Jean Stafford pays homage to literary mentors such as Ford Madox Ford ("Truth in Fiction"), documents the dawning of her literary vocation ("Miss McKeehan's Pocketbook") and bemoans what she sees as popular culture's destruction of the English language ("Men, Women, Language, Science and other Dichotomies"). What emerges from my chronological ordering of Stafford's essays is, I hope, a portrait of a developing literary artist who saw herself as a product of a particular time and place, but who felt increasingly alienated from the trends and fads of contemporary life.

An Etiquette for Writers

Being here in this room on this campus in this town that confronts these particular mountains and these queer Flatirons is no simple or perfunctory act for me. I speak of more than my habitual and crippling stage-fright and of more than my normal writer's queasiness whenever I am far away from my typewriter and my work-in-progress. I speak of an additional—and a more disabling—impediment. Here and now I am hobbled by sentiment and I am beset at every turn by a multitude of associations; for in returning to Boulder after many years, I have returned to scenes and landmarks that are more familiar to me than any later ones can ever be, more acutely meaningful since it was amongst them that, for all practical purposes, my history had its beginnings. The churches of the town, its graveyards, the junctions of its streets, the buildings of the University, the gullies of the foothills, all these are reliquaries crammed with mementoes of finished enthusiasms, heartbreaks, astonishments, intrigues, revelations, shames and terrors. For I lived here through crucial years, from the time I was ten and wore a hideous haircut and was tearfully inept in Palmer Method at the University Hill School and still believed in the spanking machine, until I was twenty-one and, after many humiliating failures to do so, finally passed enough hours of Physical Education to entitle me to receive a diploma in Macky Auditorium.

Those are years when the palates of our faculties are clean and vernal and we urgently and directly take in the shape and the color, the sound and the smell and the feeling of the physical world and can, without groping for the word, name the name of our sensation or emotion. They are not the richest years, for the greenhorn intellect is still tactless and unequivocal and cannot yet recognize ambiguity or nuance or paradox or overtone or continuity. Nor can the heart, rigid with the puritan

Excerpted from a speech given at the 1952 Writers' Conference in the Rocky Mountains. Reprinted by permission of the Jean Stafford Collection, Special Collections Department, University of Colorado at Boulder Libraries, and by permission of Russell & Volkening, Inc., as agents for the author. Copyright © 1952 by Jean Stafford.

righteousness of youth, distinguish clearly between the vexatious and the unforgivable or between the pleasant and the adorable. It is not a tolerant time of life, but it is a time of rather great and reckless integrity; we have gone headlong to the roots of the matter if we have not yet discovered the heart of it. The helmets and the masks, the arms and the armor that we take on later protect and socialize us but they also disguise; and with such cumbersome paraphernalia, our route is necessarily roundabout. I look back upon those years of my own life with certain admiration and with certain embarrassment and with no desire whatever to live them over again. I am glad that I was once obliged to be intransigent, but I am even more glad that I am now mollified and slowed down by the obliquities of middle age. But if I could, I would recapture the faith that I had then.

I was in Connecticut when I got the invitation to come to this conference, three quarters of a continent away from Boulder and the University and even more distantly removed in time from my childhood and girlhood and studenthood. But feeling is not dislocated by dislocation and the years can only partly censor memory, and ever since I wrote saying that I would come, I have been attended by a vivid and vocal entourage of past experience, impressions, gratitudes, satisfactions and regrets. Each time I considered some useful and objective subject on which to speak tonight, I was deflected by the backwash of memory on which I would then drift waywardly and will-lessly, my mind's eye blind to the domesticated landscape of New England and able only to see these fierce peaks and lonely plains. Transported from this year of Ike and Mamie Eisenhower and England's new queen and Willy Sutton and Ingrid Bergman's twins and Whittaker Chambers, I was often returned in my reflections to a summer fifteen years ago when, instead of standing behind a lectern, I sat out there, listening, on different evenings, to John Crowe Ransom, and Ford Madox Ford and John Peale Bishop and Sherwood Anderson. I was nervous to think of the change in my role from pupil to teacher, and if I had remembered what any of those writers had said, I would have cribbed shamelessly from them. But I remembered only the way they had looked and remembered the headiness of being in the presence of the practitioners of the art I had always honored above all else in life. In Connecticut, with my cat on my lap, I shivered and shook to contemplate my effrontery in coming here to state my creed, and I blushed darkly to think that in my audience there might be some of my former teachers who would still see and hear in me the gawky, wobbly, sloppy student I had been. I writhed so much I scared my cat when pitilessly I reminded myself of horrible gaffes I had made on final examinations and of boneheaded attitudes I had not had the sense to conceal.

But I could not dwell in any year or any mood for long; at one moment I saw myself in the stacks of the library lip-reading eleventh-century religious poems and taking notes for my master's thesis, each page of which was to bear at the bottom a dense frieze of *op cits* and *ibids* intended to convey an air of erudition; but the next moment I was eleven years old and was learning how to shuffle cards under the tutelage of a gifted friend who knew six different kinds of solitaire. There might abruptly stand before me isolated, out of its context, the fact that the Earl of Oxford had once called Sir Philip Sidney a puppy, but before I could detain this interesting piece of gossip and learn why I had preserved it all these years, it was obliterated and replaced by the razzmatazz of an early Hallowe'en party when I was thrillingly frightened out of seven years' growth by a bird from the ninth grade, dressed up to represent a mummy, who shook my hand with a chamois glove filled with wet corn meal. Or again, on the heels of my recollection of the first Shakespeare play I ever saw when the Ben Greet players came to town in *Macbeth*, there came, with almost equal interest, the image of a yellow trolley car that used to proceed carefully down from the top of Mapleton Hill and up University Hill until it reached the Chautauqua and there it paused, exhausted, for a long and silent time while the conductor and the passengers got out and ritualistically drank at the water fountain in the shelter house as if this were a spa and they had taken a trolley ride to a cure.

Thinking, then, of Boulder and of my sources here—the book-learning all mixed up with beefsteak fries and famous snowstorms, the scandals of the town and gown confused—thinking thus of Boulder, I felt a commingling of affection and revulsion, emotions that did not cancel one another out but coexisted in a disharmony so intense and so exhilarating and so burdened with my own early and late history, that I concluded at last it would be impossible for me to speak here with academic detachment of the art of the novel, or the state of the novel, or the future of the novel, or the novelist and society, or the novelist and psychoanalysis. I knew that I should be able to do little more than peregrinate amongst personal meanders. At first this seemed a cheat, for my audience presumably would come to learn how to write and publish books and not to listen to my reminiscences. But still, these are the pastures where my imagination feeds and since I believe that memory is one of the writer's most useful tools, perhaps I can extend and shape some of my souvenirs into precepts. Anyhow, I could not, in Boulder or anywhere else, give a recipe for writing a novel because there is none; I have heard that there are now on sale such things as "plot dictionaries" which must surely be supplemented by "character directories" and "setting atlases" and "mood guides." I have also heard of machines that not only compute difficult sums and do square root but in addition can compose musical themes; I have no doubt that they will eventually carry their impertinence to the point of parsing sentences and from there it will be no step at all to writing fiction. But I trust these automatic Quiz Kids will remain a minority group and that their work will be nothing more than a flash in the pan, and that most of the writing we will read will still be home-made and will come from people who learn how to write through a less arithmetical kind of trial and error and who, through their striving toward an excellence and an originality of expression, will dedicate themselves honestly and with love and in faith to the tradition of English letters.

I do not remember a time, after I learned the alphabet, when I did not want to write. I had no axes to grind and no crusades to lead when I was six, but I pledged allegiance to the English language at about that time and my chauvinism has been steadfast ever since. My education is abysmally defective for I could never learn to do a single thing but read and write, partly, I suppose, because it never occurred to me that anything else was of the slightest consequence. By the time I did see that other matters were integral to the perpetuation of the world, it was too late: my nervous patterns were all used up and against almost all other branches of learning, I had a pathogenic and ineradicable phobia.

I do not think that in the beginning I looked on writing as a "profession," and certainly I did not think of it as "work." I wrote for my own amusement—as Miss Kathleen Windsor was recently adjudged in court to have written *Forever Amber*, making her thus eligible for an income-tax refund on the grounds that her revenue had derived from play, not work. I did, however, require an audience and when I could not get a human member of my family to listen to me read aloud my plays and ballads and my short, short, short stories, I read them to our patient dog who loved me. I believe I must have imagined a writing career to be a perpetually happy state of mind or a serene *modus vivendi*, lived out on a high, pure Olympus whose summit was reached on wings. I had not heard of Sisyphus then nor did I know that nine tenths of one's travel is by shank's mare. When I began my first novel in the seventh grade, a thriller set in the British Museum, I was not yet concerned with the economics of my calling and the thought of publication never crossed my mind: my intention, in this book, from its first page to its twelfth and final page, was absolutely chaste and uncommercial. I typed it all out in upper case letters on the biggest and oldest and loudest typewriter ever seen, which came into my possession briefly in some way I have now forgotten. I filled in the punctuation by hand with colored pencils and I bound the manuscript with cardboard and tied it with white rick-rack. For a long time I read it over at least once a day with undiminishing reverence. I am under the impression that someone else—besides the dog—read it and said at the time that I had talent, but I am not at all sure that I was not my own discoverer.

For at least the first half of my life, I was unaware that writing was a "business," as big and complicated and ramified as the automobile or the movie industries. Nor that its society was as stratified as that of ancient Rome. Nor did I have the faintest inkling that before I was to reach the age of franchise, the "cacoethes scribendi" which even early in the eighteenth century Addison had described as being "as epidemical as the small pox" was, in our century, to be as common as the common cold. As I began to learn about starvation among writers and cold attics, consumption, debtor's prisons, dope, drink, madness, I began to suspect that writers' lives were not automatically all fun and games. But I made no personal application of my suspicion and I went on being ignorant that throughout this enormous nation, hundreds upon hundreds of my coevals in situations similar to mine were plotting novels and plotting their lives exactly as I was doing. Not knowing that I was entering a business, I did not ever dream that competition was going to be so fierce. Once I strayed for a few minutes into the thought of being an acrobatic dancer because I had learned to turn a third-rate handspring, but I abandoned the idea because I naively imagined that the field was overcrowded.

I went on never having heard of Madison Avenue, called "Ulcer Gulch" by cynical underlings in publishing houses, called, sometimes, by the more sanguine and higher salaried officers, "the Street." I did not know about the importance of having or of not having an agent— a condition that is debated until the cows come home at literary cocktail parties and on the commuting trains to Westchester and Fairfield counties. I had never heard of an option or a contract, of Scandinavian rights or west-coast representatives or clipping bureaus or promotion campaigns or book-and-author lunches. For a long time, of course, I thought that all writers were dead but even after I discovered that they were not, I did not think they were ever on view. The first writer I ever saw was Robert Frost and I saw him up close in the dining room of a small lodge in Boulder Canyon where I had been hired as a maid-of-all-works the summer I was twelve. He ordered a glass of milk to drink with his lunch and I was so light-headed that when I was cutting a lemon for his companion's iced tea, I nicked my finger nastily and a drop of my blood fell into the poet's glass. I gave it to him just as it was—it didn't show much and this romantic transfusion gave me something to think about when I was kept awake at night by pack-rats gallivanting through the attic over my head.

Perhaps my most innocent notion was that when writers talked "shop," they talked of writing, for by the time I had got to college and had gravitated toward others of my persuasion, this is what we did.

In my last year at the university, I was a member of a small group who wrote and hoped eventually *really* to write and who, making no bones about it, called ourselves "the intelligentsia." We had no sponsorship and no organization and our meetings were sporadic. But once every week or so we gathered together on the mezzanine of a melancholy sandwich-and-beer establishment on 13th Street, long since replaced by something smarter, where, for the Mermaid Tavern's hock or sack, we substituted attenuated and legal three point two. Occasionally we read aloud from our own work, but for the most part we read from the writers we had just discovered: Joyce, Proust, Pound, Eliot, Lawrence, Gide, Hemingway, Faulkner. Our prejudices were vitriolic and our admirations were rhapsodic; we were possessive, denying to anyone outside our circle the right to enjoy or to understand *The Wasteland* or *Swann's Way* or *A Portrait of the Artist as a Young Man*. We were clumsy and arrogant and imitative, relentlessly snobbish and hopelessly undiscriminating. We did not know where we were at but wherever it was, we heard the thunderous music of the spheres. It made no difference at all that we were for the most part tone-deaf. Perhaps I do my friends an injustice and they were less befuddled than I, so I shall speak only for myself when I say that I was so moonstruck by the world of modern writing that had opened up before me that I saw no difference at all in the intentions of Thomas Wolfe and Marcel Proust or those of James Joyce and Thomas Mann: all of them were godly and inviolable. Contemporaneity was our principal but not our only concern: for we had also taken up Flaubert, Stendahl, Conrad, Heine, Swift, all the Russians, the English metaphysical poets, Goethe, St. Augustine, Defoe and Nietzsche. We longed as much for other centuries as we identified ourselves with our own and we existed in a state of dichotomy: the ivory tower (a phrase that did not seem tarnished to us) that we occupied was being ceaselessly assailed by the Zeitgeist (another term we found fresh and apt). In spite of our airs and posturings and greed, we were serious and we knew that ours was no golden, carefree age: we had been reared in the Depression and our sensibilities had taken on the complexion of the national dilemma; we were dependent on NYA and the FERA jobs for our books and laboratory fees; in a sense we were living on borrowed time because we knew that after our graduation we were going to have more than a spectator's knowledge of unemployment. Along with *Walden* and *Culture and Anarchy*, we read *The Theory of the Leisure Class* and Trotsky's *Autobiography*. We began to hear of anti-Semitism; Hitler began to show that he was more than a nut; and presently the Spanish revolution was to begin, giving us the foretaste of the sanguinary confusion that has deformed the world for thirteen years.

But hope and energy and political illiteracy safeguarded us against any real emotional involvement with these issues and while we heard the Zeitgeist wail and rattle our windowpanes, we stayed snug a while in that mild, crepuscular saloon and quoted *Sweeney among the Nightingales*. So long as there are students, so long as there are writers-in-the-making, there will be these microcosms, varying according to the wars that are being fought and the intellectual vogues that are in style. We cut our baby teeth on the repercussions of the Sacco and Vanzetti trial as a new generation has cut its on Alger Hiss.

Although we, the intelligentsia of the University of Colorado, occasionally talked of the responsibility of the writer to his society and debated whether he was ethically obliged to mirror his times, we did not think in ulterior terms of reform or revolution or restoration. We were incontrovertibly single-minded and thought only in terms of writing. The play was the thing, or the poem was or the novel or the story. And because we did not yet know anything much about psychoanalysis beyond a smattering of its vocabulary, we did not investigate the morbid reasons for our impulses to write; we would have been shocked and disbelieving if anyone had even jokingly suggested that we were disinterring and exposing derangements and unwholesome desires. We may often have doubted our talent and despaired of our ability to perform, but our motives for writing never came into question. It is to the luxury and freedom of that immediate, unrealistic and simple fervor that I look back with such longing. A fervor that cools, willy-nilly, when the practical ends of writing come to subordinate the aims of it.

The Zeitgeist at last blows the tree too hard and down comes cradle and baby and all. Eight years after I left Boulder, a propitious wind knocked me down to earth where I landed on my feet in clover and if, later on, I found that the clover was an ersatz wartime substitute for the real thing, it served me for a time. For luckily my first book came out in 1944, a halcyon year for the purveyors of anything and everything since the whole nation was on a spending spree, buying everything that was on sale, including novels. In comparison to other books that came out at that time, mine had a feeble career, but from the periphery, I could see the workings of the "book business" in which it was sometimes difficult to tell whether writing was its raison d'être or was, on the contrary, its product or commodity. For example, once at a cocktail party I met a literary agent who maintained a stable of impressively thriving novelists and who had been told by our host that I had been published in a few magazines that operated on budgets that were modest almost to the vanishing point. He looked coldly at me and coldly said, "A writer has to make a lot of money to interest an agent." . . .

For writing is a private, an almost secret enterprise carried on within the heart and mind in a room whose doors are closed; the shock is staggering when the doors are flung open and the eyes of strangers are trained on the naked and newborn; one's doubts and misgivings and fears should be allowed to rest in sick-room quiet for a while. The experts may proceed to the examination but the parent should not be asked to make any further contribution. Let me quote again from M. Maurois to show what happened to Miss Windsor:

> Success was swift and spectacular. Kathleen Windsor was sent out by her publishers on an autographing tour of America, attended banquets, spoke over the radio and became a target for newsmen everywhere. They weren't always favorable. Unwisely she confessed that she had written for fame and money. Byron had learned the costly lesson that one doesn't get away with such remarks, even when true. Kathleen Windsor, it should be noted, had many other reasons for writing a novel. Among them were two: a deep-seated inferiority complex, and a painful need of public expression. These,

though, she avoided mentioning. They were kept well hidden within her. But whenever she heard a vicious joke about Amber, she was likely to cry.

I will elide this generous Frenchman's avuncular psychiatry only pausing to observe that I cannot believe Miss Windsor's inferiority complex will be cured by his announcement and that the "painful need for public expression" can hardly be called singular in a writer or, indeed, in any specimen of *homo sapiens*. Now chivalrous as his exegesis is, it is an exegesis of the creator and not of the creation and this putting of the cart before the horse is symptomatic of what is wrong today in this wide-spread vulgarization and personalization of writing, this confounding of it with another kind of activity altogether. In recent years we have seen the birth and flourishing of literary reputations months and sometimes even years before the writers to whom they belong ever appear in print. They have acquired a solid status on the strength of their intention, on their charm and their wit and their presentableness at dinner parties; in some cases, it seems almost superfluous for them to publish at all. I know of a man who has been called a writer all his life—and he is nearing sixty—who has, nevertheless, published nothing except an excerpt from his "forthcoming novel" in an obscure and ephemeral magazine. On hearing that he had gone to the country to finish his book, a canard that began at least twenty years ago, a friend of mine said, "Oh, really? What is he reading?" It is a full-time job to be a non-practicing writer and I suppose that it is an honorable enough profession but it should get itself a new name. The tunes one sings for one's supper must be neither sour nor stale; the news in the gossip columns is short-lived and must therefore continually be replenished and this necessitates ever widening one's social orbit, continually revealing just enough and not too much of what is significant in one or what is original and appealing. It is quite as profitable to appear in *Town and Country* in a photograph that includes Mrs. Harrison Williams or the Duchess of Windsor as it is to be noticed favorably in the book pages.

I do not mean to imply that I disapprove of the praise and the petting of writers nor that we should not get the same worldly rewards that people in other professions do, but I object to our being treated— and our allowing ourselves to be treated—as performers and being transferred from our bailiwick into an element in which we cannot possibly be at home. It does not follow that because we can write, we can also speak over the radio or that we will "televise" well. Nor does it follow that because I can write a book about an unhappy woman reared in the twentieth century I am therefore qualified to make a five-hundred word statement for a symposium in a women's magazine on why modern women are more unhappy than those of the nineteenth century.

As I talk, I realize that my viewpoint is probably parochial and that beyond the borders of New York's narcissistic pool, readers do not bother much about the private opinions and the private habits of the writers they read. Still I have been asked, in Bloomington, Indiana, in Greensboro, North Carolina, in Wiscasset, Maine, whether I write in long-hand or on the typewriter, whether writing is easy or hard for me, what it is in my spiritual composition that makes it impossible for me to write happy stories. And it was from Texas that there came to me a lengthy questionnaire drawn up by someone who was compiling statistics on the feeding and working habits of free-lance writers in preparation for a college thesis. On the first page, I was peremptorily asked to give my age, birthplace and the details of my education. I was then asked whether I managed just to eke out a living, whether I lived well or whether I lived luxuriously and could afford to take trips. Was I married? If so, what did my husband do? Did I contribute to his support? Could I afford a secretary? What, exactly, was my income? What had it been when I started out? Did I write at home or where? During the day or night? Morning or afternoon? Did I smoke while writing? What did I smoke? Drink while writing? What did I drink? Did I think best lying down, sitting down or on my feet? Did I need a snack during each break to give me energy to go on? If so, what did I eat? Did I prefer to write in a large room or in a small area? How much in 1951 did I deduct from income taxes for expenses? How many rejections per story or article did I usually have before placing it? Was I glad I was a free-lance writer?

I did not return the questionnaire but saved it in a file marked "Frights" but if I had I would have given this nosy Parker something to put in his pipe and smoke. I could have told him that my royalty statement from Houghton Mifflin in 1951 for a story appearing in one of the O'Brien collections was one fifteenth of a cent. I could have made him sit up and take notice by saying that I always write in my bare feet, that I am a mouth-breather during composition and that I do my best work immediately after my hair has been washed. These facts, I think, are quite as pertinent to the process of writing as the time of day I sit down at my typewriter. . . .

No serious writer takes any of this seriously. There is no need at all to expose oneself; keeping oneself before the public eye is, I think, totally unessential: we do not get forgotten so quickly nor so completely as actors and orators do and since our media are not remotely similar, we should not try to compete with them. Writers should write and their books should be read, but on the whole they should not be seen.

And I would be practicing what I am preaching if it had not seemed to me time to come back to Boulder to review the scenes of my origin and to thank my teachers for nourishing the better aspects of my better character.

Truth in Fiction

If we [writers] are worth our salt, we're scared, and a good deal of the time we should be. But some of the time we're scared of scarecrows—we're scared of fashion: do we parse in the grammars of Freud or Camp or *The New York Review of Books*? From one moment to the next we don't know whether it's "in" or "out" to be afraid of Virginia Woolf. . . .

The only way to disperse these hobgoblins is to write for yourself and God and a few close friends, and if you meet the exacting demands of this group and get their imprimatur, you can devote your whole attention to the really important agony of getting through a writing day. . . .

The most interesting lives of all, of course, are our own and there is nothing egotistic or unmannerly in our being keenly concerned with what happens to us. If we did not firmly believe that ours are the most absorbing experiences and the most acute perceptions and the most compelling human involvements, we would not be writers at all, and we would, as well, be very dull company.

But it is not fair to buttonhole our readers with a diagnosis of ourselves if there is the slightest risk of his being bored or embarrassed or offended. And while autobiography is inevitable, we must winnow carefully and add a good portion of lies, the bigger the better. . . .

When I was a young woman, I had the good fortune of talking from time to time with Ford Madox Ford who, with the generosity that made him beloved of his literary waifs, read and criticized my aimless short stories and the inchoate chapters of novels that died unborn. One time, he found some character disproportionately nasty and he asked me how closely I had drawn him from life. I said I had been as sedulous as I knew how and Ford said, "That's impolite and it's not writing fiction." He went on to observe that the better one knows one's dramatis personae, the harder it is to limn them in fiction because there is too much material, there are too many facets to tell the truth about,

Reprinted from *Library Journal* 91 (1966). Stafford, Jean. Copyright © 1966 by Reed Publishing, USA.

there are whole worlds of variants and inconsistencies that won't work and will snag the narrative. Objectivity teeters and can collapse when one judges the character on the created page the same way he does in the drawing room. Anyhow, it is not the business of the writer to judge—that is the business of the reader. The writer should not say, "This man is a villain and you must believe me because I have known him all my life." Unless you show forth his iniquities, the reader may not find him iniquitous at all, not armed with the knowledge that the brute made scurrilous observations on the size of the author's feet in the sixth grade. . . .

[O]ne evening I began reading the Holmes-Laski correspondence that had just come out and I found therein the kernel of a story ["A Reasonable Facsimile"] that I began to write the next morning. In it, Mr. Justice is a retired professor of philosophy at a western college and Harold Laski is a bright, pushy whelp who teaches at an obscure finishing school in Florida. I cannot tell you how many people have been positively identified as my wholly fictitious Holmes and Laski. . . .

Writers are rag-pickers and squirrels and they never really throw anything away. One of the great charms of writing is that of one day coming across a scene or a situation or a character that you'd put in the cupboard long ago because at the time it didn't fit.

The Felicities of Formal Education

Today, I would like to begin by musing on what I think a liberal education should be, or, rather to bring the matter to my own back door, what I wish my education *had been*. It is with very considerable trepidation that I launch upon these stormy waters because I am myself so precariously educated. Indeed, in terms of present day curricula, I am barely literate: for I have never read sociology nor have I had academic courses in sex or in the psychology of revolution or in the ethics and economics of the women's liberation movement. And, above all, I have never studied *education*. I have read very little science, and all through my schooling, I was so adroit at weaseling out of physical training that corporeally I have worn a dunce cap all my life. I grieve the last two deficiencies in my upbringing—science, that is, and sports. Convinced that I could never master mathematics after a couple of tormenting years of algebra and plane geometry, and mortally afraid of being ridiculed on a tennis court, I early on took a stand that was stereotypical in my day, that art was in some way superior to science, and that the discobolus would be out of place in Minerva's temple. . . .

In very many ways, therefore, because of my want of training in the school of opportunity or the school of hard knocks, I don't know which, I am isolated from the world about me even though my ivory tower ish rocked at its very foundations. . . .

It is, no doubt, a pleasure to be able to read the Greek and Latin poets, philosophers, and historians in the original, but very few persons so educated in the past "kept up" their Greek and Latin after leaving school. Its real value was something quite different. Anybody who has spent many hours of his youth translating into and out of two languages so syntactically and rhetorically different from his own, learns something about his mother tongue which I do not think can be learned in

Excerpted from an unpublished typescript of a lecture delivered at Barnard College in 1971. Reprinted by permission of the Jean Stafford Collection, Special Collections Department, University of Colorado at Boulder Libraries, and by permission of Russell & Volkening, Inc., as agents for the author. © 1971 by Jean Stafford.

any other way. For instance, it inculcates the habit, whenever one uses a word, of automatically asking, "What is its exact meaning?"[1] The people who have really suffered since a classical education has become "undemocratic" are not the novelists and poets—their natural love of language sees them through—but all those like politicians, journalists, lawyers, the man-in-the-street, etc. who use language for everyday and nonliterary purposes. . . . Mark Twain talks in *Roughing It* about a guide he and his brother once took into the gold fields of Nevada who plucked big words out of the blue and stuck them into his conversation wherever he thought they were likely to make an impression. The mule hauling their tools and provisions began to show signs of exhaustion and the guide observed, "Mules become bituminous from long deprivation," and on another occasion when they had camped by an alkaline lake and the tenderfoot Clemens brothers had made coffee, the guide declined, saying, "That water's too technical for me." . . .

I came from a family of readers—I was read to as a child and, like all pre-television children, as soon as I could read to myself, there was very little else I wanted to do. When I was called to supper in the middle of *Hans Brinker*, I was as cross as a bear and I'd say, "Just let me finish this chapter," and then, as often as not, I cheated and went on to the next one. . . .

If I were to be reborn—knowing as much as I do now—and had been able from the womb to direct my mother in such a way that she would pay attention and obey, I would insist that as soon as I had learned my native tongue, I would immediately be introduced to history. I am not sure where I would like to begin, whether with the settling of this continent by the immigrants from Europe and the British Isles, or with the arrival forty thousand years ago with [*sic*] the Asian hunters following the mammoth and the buffalo. Needless to say, the histories of science, of music and painting and architecture and religion would be concomitant to the chronicles of dynasties and dominions. And then there would be the mathematics and the languages and chemistry and systematic Botany, and enough economics so that I could understand why Wall Street goes off its rocker when a president enters Walter Reed for a gall-bladder operation. In the summertime I would study shop, basic plumbing, and animal husbandry. This education would take between twenty-five and thirty years and cost about a million dollars, but it would be a grand lark to look back on in my old age.

Note

1. This and the preceding sentence (beginning "Anybody who has spent . . .") are attributed to W. H. Auden by Jean Stafford in her later published essay "Men, Women, Language, Science and Other Dichotomies" *Confrontation* 7 [1973]: 71). In this unpublished typescript, however, there are no quotation marks and no attribution to Auden.—Ed.

Men, Women, Language, Science and Other Dichotomies

In lamenting my own inadequacy in physics and chemistry and biology, I have put the cart before the horse in my proposal for an ideal education. Because it is upon the knowledge of language that knowledge itself depends. And the proper teaching of language should be of prime concern from the kindergarten through the graduate school. . . .

I regret that I can no longer read Vergil and Livy, but I am glad that I once could—even though I read them badly. I learned far more of English grammar in Latin classes than I did in English classes and it was *entirely* through the study of Latin that I learned the origins and evolution of English words. In my ideal curriculum, I would demand at least four years of Latin, preferably begun in the latter years of elementary school. I am aware that a pretty strong argument could be built up against Latin since it is "dead," and therefore, to use a most offensive catch-all term "irrelevant," and it is true that its literature can be appreciated as well in good translation as in the original. But if the student will have nothing to do with Latin, then, let him study French or Spanish, Italian or German and he will begin to see, to his delight, the formation and the principles common to the family of Indo-Germanic languages of which English is the richest and the most flexible of modern specimens. It is also the most endangered: sadistic advertisers persuade the inattentive that solecisms are acceptable— Winston tastes good like a cigarette should. And the Pentagon daily coins a brand new neologism not worth a plugged nickel—"Vietnamize." Are we going to bomb the language too?

From Jean Stafford, "Men, Women, Language, Science and Other Dichotomies," first published in *Confrontation* 7 (1973): 69–74, Long Island University. Reprinted by permission.

Miss McKeehan's Pocketbook

The crying, thirsting, burning need of my life when I was a student was to get to Europe. To a western child, growing up and reading at the time I did, England was far more familiar than New England. Nor did New York City beguile me—I didn't give a hang about Broadway—I wanted to see Covent Garden and the British Museum. To get abroad in the darkest years of the Depression was a considerable undertaking, but I was hell-bent, and I managed it. Alas, nobody in England wanted me, and nobody in Europe whom I wanted wanted me; but Hitler wanted me and all other American students he could lay his hands on so that he could remove the scales from our eyes. Bedazzled by Thomas Aquinas and Eleanor of Aquitaine, I didn't rightly know who Hitler was or what he had in mind beyond offering me a fellowship, so I accepted his invitation and high-tailed it across the Rocky Mountains and across the Atlantic Ocean to Heidelberg where the greatest living authority on Beowulf, Herr Doktor Professor Johannes Hoopes, was lecturing. It was my aim to become a philologist. . . .

To a certain extent, I *am* a philologist, un-degreed as I am, because language is and has always been my principal interest, my principal concern, and my principal delight. . . .

In Heidelberg, tongue-tied, amazed, dumbfounded to be attending a university that had been established a century before the discovery of America, innocently drinking beer with young Brownshirts who soon would constitute the Enemy, totally at sea, I clung stubbornly to my imagined career amid the nut-brown groves of the Indo-Germanic languages. . . .

As my time in Heidelberg started running out, I wrote to Miss McKeehan, asking her to recommend me for a fellowship at Radcliffe or Bryn Mawr or some other college for brainy women. I have lost her

Excerpted from the text of a speech given to the associates of the Rare Book Room of the Norlin Library, University of Colorado, Boulder, in 1972. Published in *Colorado Quarterly* 24 (Spring 1976): 407–11. Reprinted by permission of the University of Colorado, Boulder, Colorado.

reply, but I remember it very well. She wrote that no, she would not sponsor me because I did not have the makings of a scholar. "Why don't you get married?" she said. "Or, better, why don't you write?" I had been a secret writer all my life, but I couldn't figure out how she knew that and to this day I can't. . . .

[F]or thirty years now I have been earning my living as a writer, largely because of Miss McKeehan's blunt demolition of an impossibly silly daydream. . . .

I have two studies in my house now. In the upstairs one, I am a novelist and short-story writer. I work there in the morning, generally wearing a skirt, a smock, a Windsor tie, and a wig with a black velvet bow pinned to the front of it. In the afternoon I work downstairs where I am a journalist, making the mortgage money to keep a roof over the upstairs ivory tower. Down there I wear denim trousers, a blue work shirt, laced half-boots that resemble those worn by a wardress in a Soviet penal institution, and a green visor.

Part 3

THE CRITICS

Introduction

The following selections cover more than 30 years of critical commentary on Jean Stafford's short fiction, ranging from one of the earliest critical assessments, by Ihab Hassan in 1955, to one of the most recent, by Bruce Bawer in 1988. Concluding this section are two personal reminiscences of Stafford, written after her death by her friends Dorothea Straus and Peter Taylor. I have attempted to give a range of critical stances and approaches indicative of their time periods: Olga Vickery's 1962 article, for example, places Stafford in the tradition of the great ironists who saw human nature as radically alienated; Chester Eisinger's 1963 essay links Stafford to a distinctly American literary tradition of symbolists like Hawthorne and Melville; Sid Jenson's 1973 study examines the two images of the West emerging in Stafford's fiction. Joyce Carol Oates's 1979 essay studies Stafford's contribution to the short story genre, then enjoying somewhat of a renaissance; Philip Stevick's 1981 study of postrealist fiction and the tradition preceding it compares Stafford's artfully crafted stories, with their solidly grounded portrayals of character and place, to the fiction of writers like Barth and Coover, whose fictional techniques identify them as distinctly postmodern; Melody Graulich's 1983 article treats the archetypal male myth of the West as it is reflected in Stafford's fiction; Maureen Ryan's 1987 critical study of the entire Stafford canon places her in a distinctly female literary tradition. Interspersed with the criticism are reviews of *Bad Characters* and *Collected Stories*, by Jerome Mazzaro, Guy Davenport, and Mary Hegel Wagner which ironically note both Stafford's reluctance to incorporate broad social or philosophical issues of her day into her fiction and the corresponding timelessness her work evokes. Without exception, critics praise Stafford's searingly honest portrayals of human nature, her deft and sensitive use of language, her incisive wit. More contemporary critics also note her links with other women writers who treat women's powerlessness and marginality in a patriarchal culture. Inevitably, each literary generation reenvisions and

107

recontextualizes the work of earlier writers, finding in the work of literary artists like Jean Stafford signs of their own cultural and social predicament. The fact that readers and critics continue to discover and admire Jean Stafford's fiction testifies to her abiding capacity to entertain, surprise, and illuminate.

Ihab Hassan

In a decade at which we still prefer to look askance, the work of Jean Stafford has rarely failed to call some attention to itself. Her incisive talent, her style so often distinguished, would indeed merit no less. Yet the attention Miss Stafford has won for her work is not all that one should like it to be: it is the kind of attention that takes her limitations for granted, that makes too much of them by accepting them too readily.

The achievement of Miss Stafford, though still in progress (and though time likes nothing better than to give a critic the lie) has an air both of freshness and orthodoxy. One feels that she has allied herself with a large tradition of the novel, the tradition of Proust and James most markedly, and with a tradition certainly not less native than Willa Cather's or Katherine Anne Porter's, while others—possibly Flaubert and Jane Austen and Dostoyevsky—stand from a distance silently on guard. Large as this tradition may appear (Miss Stafford does not seem to betray the specialness of a Paul Bowles or a Peter Taylor) a rather definite, and perhaps finite, animating center is recognizable in her fiction. The center, I think, is a metaphor of age and childhood, a composite image of change and experience, caught in an ironic, elegiac, and retrospective vision. It is her attachment to this center that defines the expense of her style and the scope of her sensibility.

Yet it is perhaps as a short story writer that Miss Stafford is best known. One feels that her sensibility, always sudden and mordant, is more happy within the confines of the shorter medium which Frank O'Connor aptly described as a "lyric cry in the face of destiny." The metaphor of childhood is expanded in such stories as "A Summer Day," "The Violet Rock," "The Healthiest Girl in Town," "The Shorn Lamb"; the metaphor of age in "The Hope Chest," "The Present," "Life Is No Abyss"; and the ironic vision in "The Maiden," "A Modest Proposal," "Children Are Bored on Sunday," and "Polite Conversa-

From "Jean Stafford: The Expense of Style and the Scope of Sensibility," *Western Review* 19 (Spring 1955): 185–203. Reprinted by permission of the author. © by Ihab Hassan.

tion." But to speak of an expanded metaphor is to state the achievement of some thirty stories almost too simply. For if some of these stories reinforce what Miss Stafford has already presented in her three novels, and if some recapitulate it, there are others, notably in the collection *Children Are Bored on Sunday*, 1953, which lead us beyond all previous echoes to vantages from which as she herself put it, "the convolutions and complexities of human relationships, . . . the crucifixions and the solaces of being alive," may be viewed anew. To particularize these, to give them hue and life, to locate them in the realities of our world is the intent of her fiction.

The hysteria of loneliness and imagination in the plight of Ramona Dunn, "fat to the point of parody," against the baroque setting of Heidelberg, in "The Echo and the Nemesis"; the slow estrangement and hopeless retrenchment of the couple in "A Country Love Story," on a wintry scene; the depersonalization of childhood amidst the arid Indian reservation atmosphere of "A Summer Day"; the betrayal and confusion of the spirit on a bleak Ash Wednesday morning, "Between the Porch and the Altar" of St. Patrick; the callousness of human intercourse among prurient residents and divorcées visitors of a Caribbean island, in "A Modest Proposal," bring from many corners snatches of high lucidity. Two of the best stories in this collection, though they deal with adults rather than children, reveal two different attitudes Miss Stafford likes to adopt towards her subject. "The Interior Castle," in which style is transfixed with meaning, captures the acute reality of consciousness: pain and wonder, void and sensation, the magic drama of the mind inscrutably playing the role of object and subject at the same instant of perception, eternally Narcissus, though more in Valéry's than in the classical sense. The import of the story—a girl undergoes a critical brain operation—is anything but clinical: it is that of pain made serviceable in the quest for identity: it is that of an outrage committed against what is most secret in man, perhaps the radical betrayal of life itself: "The pain was a pyramid made of a diamond; it was intense light; it was the hottest fire, the coldest chill, the highest peak, the fastest force, the furthest reach, the newest time. It possessed nothing of her but its one infinitesimal scene: beyond the screen as thin as gossamer, the brain trembled for its life, hearing the knives hunting like wolves outside, sniffing and snapping. Mercy! Mercy! cried the scalped nerves." In its strange, closed-in implication, the story merits comparison with Aiken's "Silent Snow, Secret Snow." The manner of "Children Are Bored on Sunday" is less poetic than ironic, its situation less private than social. Miss Stafford, by confronting urban with rural values, succeeds in making a rather subtle comment on the enervated, disinherited New York intellectual who likes to see himself as "Pontius Pilate, that hero of the untoward circumstance," and who, without his stylized gossip and party rituals, succumbs to boredom and despair on a symbolic Sunday between the museum stroll and the solitary martinis. One feels, however, that the author has risen here to a larger view of her two characters, for the unhappiness of Emma like that of Eisenburg has a depth to which satire alone cannot penetrate.

In point of structure, the stories hold some affinities with a type we commonly associate with the *New Yorker*, though they hold more, when at their best, with the tradition of Joyce and Chekov. The intimate glimpse unresolved, the moment of sudden knowledge, the reversal of a situation, the symbolic crisis, the humor of innocence and perversity, find each some deft application in Jean Stafford's stories. The technique aims, I think, at an effect most nearly presentational: an act is largely apprehended as implication and an event as pure experience. But drama will not suffer itself to be shut out. It is present in the best of these stories under the guise of irony, a kind of irony which, in any particular conflict, is made more valuable by Miss Stafford's attitude of simultaneous criticism towards all characters engaged in that conflict. Such an attitude endows each character with a reality separate from his author's and allows the irony of one point of view to be dramatically modified by that of another—"A Country Love Story," "The Maiden," and "A Modest Proposal" are examples. The symbolic object, a prominent device in these stories, often serves to heighten the ironic development: the change to which it submits in the character's eyes is a part of the more significant change in the total situation—the sleigh, the two decanters, and the figure of Pan in the three preceding stories submit to this kind of transformation.

When the stories fall short of their intent, it is usually because too much is made of too little, "The Present" or the satiric conception is too simple, "Polite Conversation" or the style is too cumbrous, "Life Is No Abyss"—a story otherwise effective; or the Gothic touch is in parts too heavy, "The Bleeding Heart." But perhaps the most serious lapse to which a writer like Miss Stafford is susceptible is the one Frank O'Connor had in mind when he wrote, "It is one of the weaknesses of the story-writer that, because of his awareness of the importance of the crisis, he tends to inflate it, to give it artificial symbolic significance."

The expense of style and the scope of sensibility. It is perhaps time to pick up again a phrase which is intended both as judgment and summary. For to define the quality of Jean Stafford's style and sensibility, to find the scope and the expense of each, is, I believe, to grasp the substance of her achievement in contemporary letters. It is an achievement based on pattern and some internal coherence, reenforced by its distinctive motifs, and developing still towards a larger order. Miss Stafford's childhood in California, her adolescence in Colorado, the year in Germany, the time she spent in New York, and particularly her life in New England are all reflected in her fiction with an authenticity that goes beyond regionalism to that immense viability which is American life.

But the pattern of fiction is not of places, it is rather of words and passions. Words and passions, style and sensibility—the terms seem to follow us about. At its worst the style of Miss Stafford lacks resilience: it is brittle and brilliant, learned in chinoiseries and legerdemain. But then it is not very often at its worst and its intent redeems its failures. The intent of her style—which is sometimes also its expense—appears to be multiple: erudite in the substantive and the specific, it attempts to lodge her story in reality, to catch what James called "the relief, the expression, the surface, the substance of the human spectacle," and to justify Blake when he observed that "The Eye sees more than the heart knows"; erudite in irony and persiflage, it wants to criticize what it reveals and describes, to discover the ridiculous and grotesque, to put, as Berenson would say, in every remark some "metaphysical lining or sting"; and erudite in that inner correspondence of things which reigns in the Romantic world, it aims to weld appearance with reality as Baudelaire did in his "forests of symbols," and to render each detail in a manner that would satisfy Elizabeth Bowen when she asks for "the naturalistic surface, but with a kind of burning." But in the end it is not the style's erudition in all these respects that sustains it: it is its poetry and control, and its memorable interpretation of experience—as in *The Catherine Wheel*. So large an intent must occasionally admit of failure. Then are we left with the hiatus in narrative and perception, and that loss of dramatic presence which is the novelist's bane—as in parts of *Boston Adventure*.

The scope of Jean Stafford's sensibility may be viewed through the heightened consciousness of childhood and senescence. It includes the magic apprehension of the first and tragic retrospect of the second, a world too closed and one too open—the realities of the future and of the past converging on the critical present. A sensibility so oriented must, and does, enlist a triple vision: a psychological insight into the internal life, a panoramic view of the changeful past, and an ironic sense of that unremitting tension between the internal and external in the life of man.

Miss Stafford's opinions on the uses to which psychology may be put in literature are voiced in an admirable essay, "The Psychological Novel," and need little theoretic qualifications.[1] She says that "Because Proust is an artist, his novel transcends its techniques and is a novel and does not smell of the clinic"; and of Freud she remarks that "He has made our moral attitudes more humane and he has modified our habits of observation." It is precisely these two statements that I should like to hold up to *The Mountain Lion* by way of delimiting a more general problem: the psychological rendering of human tragedy. For the novel, like some of Miss Stafford's stories, and unlike *The Catherine Wheel*, does not seem to me fully to transcend its techniques, nor does its conflict appear to be the more moral for its humanized psychology. The point is worth making, not because the danger it implies is insurmountable—Miss Stafford does surmount it in her felicitous moments—but rather because its implication puts some limit on the significance of tragedy in the modern world. The frailty of love which Capote and Carson McCullers sometimes emphasize seems almost to exempt their characters from responsibility; in a writer like Colette, "abnormal" as her situations are, that exemption from morality, which some take the pathological ward to abbet, is hardly implied. As to the panoramic view of the past, it is, I do believe, a contingent of the novelist's art itself; not the dimension of Proust alone, but of every writer of fiction since Fielding. "There is only one time," Miss Stafford has Katharine say, "and that is the past time. There is no fashion in *now* or in *tomorrow* because the goods has not been cut"; and again, "there was no progression in time because there was no perspective and therefore no shrouding of the past; the present was exactly the same size as the past and of exactly the same importance and except in the most minor and mechanical of ways, the future did not seem to exist." It is this gravid sense of time, the penetration of experience into memory, that Miss Stafford awakens; for hers is a sensibility attuned to the rhythm of change, the arch drama, both in the life of her characters and in their ambient realities. The social force impinges on the refractory substance of the soul: this is what both Trilling and Schorer have recognized to be the life of the novel. And it is to reconcile these that

Jean Stafford resorts to the ironic vision, perhaps the only vision that could reconcile Jane Austen to Dostoyevsky in the world we know. The conflict of time with itself, the present with the past, the future with the present, further generates that conflict of social values of which *one* manifestation, in Trilling's words, is "the tension between a middle class and an aristocracy which brings manners into observable relief as the living representation of ideals and the living comment on ideas." (So did Newman and Strether once seek a "Europe" to which they were in an innate moral sense superior; so does Sonia Marburg seek "Boston." The ideal transferred, in our time, from "Europe" to "Boston" suggests a new and interesting conception of America, a conception which Miss Stafford's "A Winter's Tale" and "The Cavalier" further enlarge.) But the conflict of class and value goes beyond the possibilities of satire: it presses too closely on "the problems of the human heart in conflict with itself." Its labour is of love and fortitude, and of the million crackling ironies that riddle our existence. And perhaps the final measure of Jean Stafford's sensibility is that still in growth, it has assumed the labor with a depth of assertiveness little credited to our new writers.

Note

1. *The Kenyon Review* (Spring, 1948).

Olga W. Vickery

Among contemporary writers Jean Stafford has merited considerable critical attention and received surprisingly little. (The only extended treatment is Ihab H. Hassan's "Jean Stafford: The Expense of Style and the Scope of Sensibility," *Western Review*, Spring, 1955.) Reviewers have pointed out her affinities with Proust, James, Austen, and Dostoevski and solemnly agreed that she is not their equal. But since not many novelists are, it is perhaps fairer and certainly more instructive to think of her in relation to such authors as Eudora Welty and Carson McCullers, both of whom have commanded far greater attention than Miss Stafford, if only by virtue of their connection with the currently fashionable South. All three are fascinated by the image of childhood and adolescence; by the misfit or freak who dramatizes isolation, loneliness, and inversion; and by the poignant quest of the individual for understanding and love. *The Member of the Wedding* echoes in mood, theme, and character *The Mountain Lion*; *The Golden Apples* and *Boston Adventure* both focus on the exclusiveness of a group, whether familial or societal; and the tormented creatures of *The Ballad of the Sad Café*, *The Heart is a Lonely Hunter*, and *Reflections in a Golden Eye* find their kin in all of Miss Stafford's novels and short stories.

At the same time there is a considerable difference in the sensibility of these three novelists. Carson McCullers has a gift for the initial perception which is also a basic one and which she enshrines in the movement of the plot. Eudora Welty, a virtuoso of style and mood, is a fabulist of the imagination. In contradistinction to both of these, Jean Stafford is firmly committed to the ironic vision of the external world of manners and the internal world of psychological process. Whatever the reason for critical neglect, then, whether her slender output or simply her failure to capture the popular imagination, it is time that a closer look was given to her novels: *Boston Adventure* (1944), *The Mountain Lion* (1947), and *The Catherine Wheel* (1950), as well as to her short

From "Jean Stafford and the Ironic Vision," *South Atlantic Quarterly*, 61:4. Copyright Duke University Press, 1962. Reprinted with permission.

stories, ten of which were collected as part of *The Interior Castle* (1953). By so doing we may discover a fictional world with manifest interest and significance for our time.

For the historical orientation of this world, Miss Stafford uses the inexorable drift towards the Second World War and its chaotic aftermath. Though she is not primarily concerned with politics, national or international, nor with the events recorded in history books, references to storm troopers, anti-Semitism, the Spanish Civil War, and the attraction of Communism convey the tensions of a world bent on its own destruction.

These dark impulses, expressed not only in individual acts but in the wholesale slaughter of battle, remain as part of war's aftermath of disorder and dislocation. The latter finds its embodiment in the alien as hero, simultaneously epical and picaresque. Like Henry James, Jean Stafford sends her characters to Europe, usually Germany, to have their illusions tested and their innocence shattered in a culture they cannot understand. Typical of these is the young American journalist in "The Maiden," who sees serenity, sensitivity, and, most important, a capacity for love in an unloving world embodied in a German lawyer and his wife, only to discover that their love had had its origin in the *totentanz*, in the sexual excitation of observing the execution of a petty criminal. The theme of an ancient evil, of guilt and disillusionment, is inextricably a part of the European adventure. Conversely, Europeans are driven by necessity or their own restlessness to become aliens in America. A German shoemaker and his Russian wife, a wealthy countess, a doctor from Heidelberg, a Hungarian landlady, their ties with Europe broken and those with America not yet established, take their place as residents of a cultural limbo where they live the marginal existence of the deracinated. . . .

Linked to the alien and the rebel is yet another figure, the freak. For what Miss Stafford refers to as "spiritual mutilation" has a physical equivalent in the symbolic scar. In contrast to the beauty and serenity of Congreve House, there is a veritable gallery of freaks—an epileptic, a monstrously fat lady, a man with an ear no bigger than a peanut, and another with no nose. Others, more normal in appearance, reveal a variety of eccentricities which never fail to fascinate Andrew Shipley and his friend, Victor Smithwick. Though not actual freaks, many of the major characters display some disfigurement, some evidence of their invisible wound. An incongruous note in the perfection of their beauty is provided by Katherine Congreve's snow white hair and by

Shura Marburg's cracked and reddened hands. More striking are the crosswork of scars on the face of the young girl in "The Interior Castle," the ugliness, at once pathetic and ludicrous, of Ralph and Molly Fawcett, the unsightly wen covered by the yellow ascot of the seemingly impeccable Bostonian in "The Bleeding Heart," and the livid purple patch on the cheek of Nathan Kadish, making him "as sensitive as if his mark were a raw sore, continually being rubbed against or hit." As long as they bear these scars, such characters are the outcasts and misfits of the human community, presenting the most extreme form of alienation possible, alienation from the self as well as the world. The image of the former is found in Ramona Dunn of "The Echo and the Nemesis" brooding over the Ariel self she had buried under layers and layers of fat, or in Pansy Vanneman of "The Interior Castle" recognizing "that she could never again love anything as ecstatically as she loved the spirit of Pansy Vanneman, enclosed within her head."

These three archetypal figures—the alien, the rebel, and the freak—serve, then, as a focus for exploring the cultural condition of the modern world. That condition is given an ethical dimension through a fusion of psychological, humanistic, and Christian terms. Moral judgment is couched in the language of Freud as well as of the Bible, and the fusion is effected through imagery. The serpent, referred to in crucial scenes of each of the novels, is equally at home in the worlds of theology and depth psychology, and possession by the devil may be construed literally or metaphorically. By seeing the eternal problem of innocence and guilt, good and knowledge, from this threefold perspective, Miss Stafford gives full scope to her ironic vision while enriching and extending her material. The use of terms, concepts, and images drawn from a variety of ideologies is the language and technique of the ironist who seeks to show both the metaphoric, incomplete character of the insights they articulate and their inability to command single-minded belief.

Caught up in this dualistic universe, the individual is necessarily involved in a never-ending conflict conducted on a multitude of levels. Dream struggles against reality, leading Rose Fabrizio of "The Bleeding Heart" to escape her own environment by inventing a story of being adopted by a cultured Bostonian whom she has seen in the public library, or the young wife in "A Country Love Story" to imagine a lover who finally becomes more real and more precious than her taciturn, suspicious husband. Those who do not retreat into "the interior castle" of fantasy are confronted with a twofold quest: the search for a unified self which will establish inner harmony and the search for love which will assure external accord. The former focuses on the moral and psychological problem of guilt arising out of the divergent pressures of desire and duty or emotion and reason. The latter quest is concerned with the social problem of the relationship between the self and others, bearing its own dichotomies of love and hate, acceptance and rejection, communion and an intensified sense of isolation. In the macabre symbolic marriage of Emma and Eisenburg of "Children are Bored on Sunday" the two quests are fused to reveal their full complexity and irony. If only for a brief time, they seek "to compare their illnesses, to marry their invalid souls for these few hours of painful communion, and to babble with rapture that they were at last, for a little while, no longer alone. Only thus, as sick people, could they marry. In any other terms, it would be a *mésalliance*. . . . If only it could take place—this honeymoon of the cripples, this nuptial consummation of the abandoned."

Chester E. Eisinger

The New Fiction Defined:
The Triumph of Art

In the forties certain novels and short stories began to appear that
critics presently identified as the "new fiction." The term is far from
satisfactory, but since nothing better offers and since it has gained a
certain currency, I shall use it. One difficulty with it is that it does not
designate a fiction that is genuinely new in any significant way. No
innovations of technique and no original ideas appear in the new fiction.
What newness it has lies in what it emphasized and what it rejected
rather than in what it originated: in concentrating its attention upon
certain thematic considerations, in rejecting social-political or philosophical ideas as the legitimate subject matter of fiction, in emphasizing
the craftsmanship of writing. Another difficulty is that the term does
not apply simply to one kind of fiction. It embraces the psychological
novel and the novel of manners, as written by Jean Stafford, for example; the desperate nihilism of Paul Bowles; the gothic decadence of
Truman Capote. What unity it has as a meaningful category is not
found in any monopoly of region or generation, for the new fiction
appears in North and South, is written in the forties by writers old and
young. Yet the new fiction *is* different, despite the variety within its
own boundaries, from anything else written in the decade. And its
difference will help us, in a positive way, to see what, essentially, it
is.

The task of defining this difference is complicated by the similarity
of the new fiction to other kinds of fiction written in the forties. It is
not an isolated phenomenon in its time. It shares with the new liberal-
ism and the conservative imagination a conviction that the end of
innocence has come to America. Lines of sympathetic understanding
run from it to the conservative imagination; they both have a high

From *Fiction of the Forties* (Chicago: University of Chicago Press, 1963), 231–33, 294–307.

119

regard for myth, tradition, a code of behavior, aesthetic form. They have a mutual ally in the new critics. Caroline Gordon and Robert Penn Warren, as critics and fiction writers, are at one with the new fiction in many respects. But they, and the new liberals too, are always conscious of an idea of society in their work and are attached to a particular idea. The new fiction is generally innocent of any such idea. Its writers want to create a pure fiction, apolitical and asocial. In this desire lies one aspect of its separateness. Since, in my judgment, no fiction is without some connection with the society in which it is created, the safe generalization about the new fiction is that it is without loyalties to any order of society and without hope for a different or better order than the one it sees. This is a second part of its separateness from both the liberal and the conservative imagination. It has no allegiance to a particular social structure. Yet in regarding society as a subject for satire or a reason for nihilistic despair, it reveals its dependence upon a social order, or disorder—the given social situation which it tends to view with contempt, or horror, or indifference. It tends to be solipsistic, but not because it regards the pursuit of the self as a sustaining quest for meaning in life, as Warren does, for example. On the contrary, the new fiction confronts the irreducible self negatively, fantastically, pessimistically.

This same ambiguity of difference within similarities extends into a consideration of the origins of the new fiction. It may be explained as having a social origin, as being a negative reaction on the part of writers in the forties to a world of such bleak confusion and hopelessness that they have had no choice but to reject it. The difficulty is that so many other writers rejected the world they lived in during the forties. The differentness of the new fiction is that it turned its back more firmly, more studiedly, more finally upon the Western world of experience and idea than others did. Yet such an observation applies more to the work of Paul Bowles than it does to that of Jean Stafford. Her novels suggest that the origins of the new fiction may be found in literary history and that it may be defined in terms of its literary progenitors. She is an authentic daughter of Henry James. To Miss Stafford the new fiction means a combination of the psychological novel and the novel of manners in work wrought with careful attention to the craft of writing, fiction in the tradition not only of James but of Edith Wharton too. The new fiction generally, to leave Miss Stafford, found in Flaubert and Joyce other masters of technique, from whom it learned the lessons of point of view, novelistic structure and dramatic action, stream of consciousness. It found in the work of Hawthorne and Melville models for the symbolic rendering of experience. Beyond technique, that work revealed the sharklike, ubiquitous evil that the writers of the new fiction found peculiarly appropriate to their time. The new fiction had available, finally, the work of Kafka, the haunted mind from Central Europe, who domesticated the alienated personality in the twentieth-century nightmare. To be sure, the new fiction shares this literary ancestry with other kinds of fiction, especially that of the conservative imagination. But these influences, regarded in their totality, play such an intense and decisive role in the new fiction as to differentiate it from all other contemporary work. . . .

The Two Worlds of Jean Stafford

Jean Stafford is the finest exemplar of the Jamesian tradition in her generation. A true daughter of James, she gathers together various strands in the fictional practice of her contemporaries, writing social satire that is reminiscent of Marquand and exploring the maturation theme as Schorer and Maxwell do. But these superficial resemblances to others do not convey the quality of the exquisite sensibility that she has dedicated to the pursuit of psychological realism in her work, an approach which James showed her the way to and which Freud, as she acknowledges, both deepened and illuminated for her. "To be writers, then," she has said, "we must be good psychologists, and this is only another way of saying that we must be experts in the study of reality and cool judges of our own natures." In this enterprise of studying and judging, writers are indebted to Freud, for he has "made our moral attitudes more humane and he has modified our habits of observation, making us more alert to our conduct and to the patterns and symbols of our experience, enriching our insights, sharpening our sense of meaning." This psychological vision, which she so intensely cultivates, is one of her chief aids in drawing the fine distinctions that characterize her work and link her in still another way with James. These distinctions arise out of her concern with the interior consciousness of her characters, where much of the action in her fiction takes place, and issue in the moral relations she establishes among her people. James and Freud join forces, then, to teach her how to see, from a psychological and moral point of view, what must be the consistent business of the novel, which is always concerned, she says, with "emotional motivations and their intellectual resolutions, with instincts and impulses and conflict and behavior, with the convolutions and complexities of human relationships, with the crucifixions and solaces of being alive."

She has had other teachers as well, to join those two, who only appear to be an odd combination. Dostoevski, whom Nietzsché regarded as a great psychologist, makes his presence felt especially in the first part of her first novel, although he has a continuing influence upon her. His special ability to summon his imaginative resources for a scene of excessive emotionalism or of erratic human behavior seemed to present Miss Stafford with a model of power in the writing of fiction. She seems also to have been moved by Dostoevski's penetration to the dark truths that lie below the surface of human reason. She knows from Dostoevski that rending mixture of love and hate in the human personality which makes for the complexities of human relationships. Although she did not mention Proust in a list of favorite authors she once compiled, her manipulation of time and her sharp awareness of the presentness of the past remind us readily of this writer. And finally she had drawn upon Jane Austen's accomplishments in the drawing room. She gives a more muscular and less disciplined account of life there than Miss Austen does, but it is nonetheless laced with the sharpness of wit and the depth of perception that so consistently marks the writings of Jane Austen.

The uses to which she puts her mixed and celebrated literary heritage are very much her own. The prevailing pattern in her fiction is to exploit a conflict in contrasting spheres of experience; her stories emerge as the fruits of the tension thus generated and of the differences thus exposed. The process is not a dialectic, because Miss Stafford is not intent upon a synthesis. But this is not to say that her fiction is static. The movement, the development, in her stories take place independently within each sphere, and sometimes simultaneously. This pattern of conflict prevails in two major areas in her work: it may take the form of a clash of cultures, or it may be seen in the division of the self represented by the conscious and the unconscious levels of human experience. The two worlds of her fiction are the social world of cultural differences and the psychic world. And within the social world are many contrasts: between national groups, Americans and Germans, for example; or between regional groups, representing New England and the West, for example; or between outsiders, like European immigrants, and insiders, like the Boston aristocracy; or between the world of the adult and the world of the child. Often, as she manages the conflicts that arise from differing cultural allegiances and moral standards, she is at the same time slipping back and forth between the conscious and unconscious minds of her characters to record in depth the impact of these conflicts. It is the carefully traced and felt intricacies of this complicated procedure that give the depth and intensity to Miss Stafford's fiction. . . .

In 1953 Miss Stafford published *The Interior Castle*, an omnibus volume which contained a collection of short stories called *Children Are Bored on Sunday*. All these had appeared between 1945 and 1950. (In the same period she published additional stories in various periodicals, but these have not yet been collected.) The stories in this volume have the brilliant surface sheen that we have come to expect from the fiction that appears in the *New Yorker*, where many of them were first published. But they are not superficial. Built around the clash of two worlds, the conscious and the unconscious as well as national or regional polarities, they reach, especially in their psychological penetration, far down into the recesses of the human personality. Sometimes one has the feeling that they are nothing more than exercises in Miss Stafford's talent for insight or for psychological empathy, as in "The Interior Castle," a concentrated study of pain which in the end is only a tour de force. In the stories involving a clash of cultures, Miss Stafford is ironic and disciplined, always giving her loyalties conditionally in recognition of the universal fallibility of man. "The Bleeding Heart" is a plant in the story of that name, but the title refers also to a Mexican girl who deludes herself, idealizes the New England character, and then must face the realities of an impoverished and decadent New Englander, who is himself something of a bleeding heart. This story, where the irony compels our perception of the difference between reality and appearance, is one of the few that presents a fully rounded form. Many are wanting in a design for the whole that gives the aesthetic satisfaction of completion. Few are astir with the moral overtones of Miss Stafford's imagination when it burns most brightly.

Charles Feidelson, Jr., has argued that modern American literature began with the turn toward symbolism in the mid-nineteenth century. Miss Stafford's work is the expression, in the forties, of that continuing tradition in which the moral life of the novel has centered in its symbolism. I have not been able to speak of her fiction without reference to

Hawthorne and Melville. Her achievement has been to carry on what they started. Finding in James a similar morality, she might have passed him over. But he offered her a different manner, and this was decisive. It is what makes her a writer of the new fiction, a writer for whom style always counts, and counts for more than it did with Hawthorne or with Melville. It is her style that is the enabling instrument in the fabrication of her irony and her symbols, that bares to us the truth of her psychological insights. She shows us, then, how the new fiction is in reality a continuation of a certain line in American fiction and has its roots in a past which still nourishes it. This is a different line from the one to which Capote and Bowles are attached, the one that runs from Poe. Seen together, the two lines place the new fiction in a proper perspective, confirm its Americanism, and demonstrate that its newness lies in making the old current.

Jerome Mazzaro

At the end of *Swann's Way*, Marcel Proust has his narrator say, "The places which we have known do not belong to the world of space, where we locate them for convenience. They were only a narrow slice among the other contiguous impressions which made up our life of that time: the memory of a certain image is only the regret of a certain instant; and the houses, the roads and the avenues are fugitive, alas! like the years." The perception of human experience, relative to the person who perceives it and to the surroundings, the moment, and the mood, may well be applied to the fiction of Jean Stafford, who, like Proust, has the remarkable tendencies to stop time and in time's stoppage to create memorable characters. For both novelists, the ultimate units of reality are events, each of which is unique and can never occur again. In the flux of the universe, these events can only form similar patterns. As Katharine Congreve, a character in Miss Stafford's novel *The Catherine Wheel* (1952), explains, "There is only one time, and that is the past time. There is no fashion in *now* or in *tomorrow* because the goods has not been cut." In this "fashion" the characters of both their worlds are betrayed by the inevitable changes of time as places alter and the past becomes as irrevocable as the peculiar moments of time in which particular events occur. And these characters, in spite of the logic of the processes by which they change, always change and finally fade away, disintegrated by illness or old age. Love, on which they counted once to stop time, changes too, and fails; and society, which at first seemed so sure, in a few years recombines its groups, merges, and transforms its classes.

For Miss Stafford the outlines of these betrayals begin with Sonie Marburg's disenchanting cinderella venture into the world of Miss Pride in *Boston Adventure* (1944) and continue through *The Mountain Lion* (1947), *The Catherine Wheel* (1952), and *Children Are Bored on Sunday*

From "Remembrances of Things Proust" (a review of Jean Stafford's *Bad Characters*), *Shenandoah* 16 (Summer 1965): 114–17. Reprinted from *Shenandoah*: The Washington and Lee University Review, with the permission of the Editor.

(1953). Their classic statement is "A Country Love Story," in which a wife, unable to win back the affections of her husband, creates an imaginary lover who in turn falls irrevocably victim to a continuum of human experience: "She knew now that no change would come, and that she would never see her lover again. Confounded utterly, like an orphan in solitary confinement, she went outdoors and got into the sleigh. The blacksmith's imperturbable cat stretched and rearranged his position, and May sat beside him with her hands locked tightly in her lap, rapidly wondering over and over again how she would live the rest of her life."

The ten stories which comprise *Bad Characters*, Miss Stafford's second collection of stories, continue these betrayals of external and internal life, of past and present, of reality and the dream. Moreover, as this discrepancy is most noticeable and painful to the aged, young lovers, and children, the stories concern one or more of these groups. In them, realism opposes romanticism; the aged find that the past cannot be relived; lovers, that their havens of happiness are infringed on; and children, that their dreams prove false; and since, like Proust, Miss Stafford is a moral relativist, what emerges is the notion that right is whatever is necessary to live at any particular moment of time, so long as it does not hurt others. Her most admirable characters go into realms of isolated dreamworlds which destroy them, and her "bad characters," as she calls them, destroy others with their imagined views of the universe.

In all these stories the limitations of Miss Stafford's Proustian approach are made too-easily apparent. Like the physicist whose view of the universe becomes more comprehensible and acceptable as he views a greater variety of events in an organic structure of interrelationships and interdependences, each involving every other and the whole, her world and its acceptability gain from an increased, gigantic, dense mesh of complicated relationships. This density is sometimes present in her novels, but of necessity diminishes in her shorter fiction where the less-complicated glimpses of life seem oversimplifications, relying upon predominant relationships. The oversimplification, most apparent in the stories like "The End of a Career" and "The Captain's Gift," coupled with her moral relativism which stresses the uniqueness of each moment, tends to increase the exaggeration, the sentimentality, and the nostalgia of her portrayals and caricature them by turning even the most casual and commonplace of her climaxes into irrevocable moments of great decision. Moreover, since the values on which these decisions are based fail to extricate themselves from situations and larger extractable morals are impossible, there tends to be in all her fiction an overemphasis by both Miss Stafford and the reader on the manner of portraying these dense relationships—her style and her characterization. In both these areas one cannot mistake her accomplishments. Her prose style is remarkable and withstands any comparison with Henry James's prose; her grasp of situation is often flawless; and her characters, even when unimportant, emerge fully-drawn.

As a result of this apparent emphasis and oversimplification, the writing in *Bad Characters* does not seem major. The reader has the feeling that Miss Stafford has not asked herself the real questions about man, that she has skirted these questions by creating unreal conflicts, or rather by stressing the moments in life when man, knowingly almost, wraps himself in unreality. In addition, for the fashion-minded reader of literature her fiction seems unaffected by the major social, intellectual, artistic, and philosophical movements since the mid-forties. Her stories, as a consequence, resemble the pasts which she steadfastly denies her characters—a pleasant regression on the reader's part into a simpler world "where grandparents on their grand tours breezed on their trust funds." This is most evident in that the oldest of the stories, "The Captain's Gift" (1946), is little different from "The End of a Career" (1956). Thus, too, the reading of her fiction like the recollection of her characters like the novels of Marcel Proust becomes a kind of contiguous remembrance of things past. Yet for any reader to dismiss her work on these grounds solely is to be naively unaware of the durability of memory.

Guy Davenport

Miss Stafford writes with a dry precision about those currents of life that run deepest in our lives and which control our most insignificant actions. In a childhood friendship she can expose the whole art of hypocrisy. In a story about a beautiful woman who is nothing but a beautiful woman she can make human vanity stand naked, helpless, caught in the act. The training of a dog reflects for her all the malevolence in the society of a small Colorado town. A cat can be made to contain the agony of a professor who has found at last what he thought he had always wanted, a devoted, adoring student—who turns out to be a petrifying bore.

These stories are built by a master's hand; no detail is wasted, no irrelevance introduced. Yet they are visually rich and fast of action. At heart Miss Stafford is a psychologist, interested to trace the influence of one mind upon another, or to show the power of an idea growing in the mind. Action is but a metaphor for ingrained thought, thought that is often ironically at variance with the best interests of its subject, or so devilishly disguised that it moves best when undetected by the mind that harbors it.

From "Tough Characters, Solid Novels" (a review of Jean Stafford's *Bad Characters*), *National Review*, 26 January 1965, 66. © 1965 by National Review, Inc. Reprinted by permission.

Mary Hegel Wagner

What, then, does she write about? Only about incidents that have happened to each of us: minor cruelties, misunderstandings, family dissension, loneliness, indifference, personal failings and character abrasions of one kind or another.

Out of these commonplaces she builds an emotional environment so that each story emerges as a harmonious entity. Above all, she is a stylist; her sentences, abstracted from the whole, are beautiful in a way that has almost become passé. . . .

If timeliness is prerequisite to art, it is debatable that Miss Stafford's work will endure. Certainly it is not representative of its age. It is not ugly, like a Campbell's Soup label. It is not iconoclastic, like the destruction of universities or the burning of cities. It is not violent, like the smashing of heads. On the contrary, it is the antithesis of all these things. It does not even share the helter-skelter, breakneck, self-confident impatience of the this-is-the-worst-of-all-possible-worlds-and-can-only-get-better-from-here-on-in school of thought. Her brooding words hold no brief for the world as it is, but neither do they indicate a hope for improvement. There is both acceptance and regret of its imperfections, with the added corollary that it is the business of the artist to depict them. So much for one side of the debate.

On the other, if timelessness is an attribute of art, then Miss Stafford may be considered a success. Monkeys will always behave like monkeys, old men like old men, and little girls like little girls. It is the recognition of our own experience that enchants us in her work, winnowed as it is through her unique perception. As long as the language of the century remains intelligible, so long the enchantment will survive.

From a review of *The Collected Stories of Jean Stafford*, *America*, April 1969, 426–27. Reprinted by permission of *America* magazine.

Sid Jenson

Jean Stafford, California born and Colorado raised, follows a long tradition of American writers who have ambivalent attitudes about East and West, about civilization and primitive nature. Miss Stafford, like Cooper, Twain, and James, has visceral and cerebral attractions which simultaneously draw her to the city and to the country. This tension creates in her fiction a dramatic depth typical of much good Western fiction.

Jean Stafford now lives in New York City, and like Henry David Thoreau, she occasionally flees from the artificial city to the natural land (to a cabin in Maine) so that she may live deliberately. But like Thoreau, she tramps back to the city to have some of mother's apple pie. She loves the country, but for an artist it is too distracting. "There are so many fine things to do,"[1] she says.

But the city, where she does most of her writing, is just as distracting. Even though she attempts to keep her city life simple, she doesn't have much luck. As she says, "It's so easy in New York to fall into the habit of going to parties. You go to one cocktail party and then find yourself making a date for another. And having lunch with someone every day. It doesn't work."[2] Jean Stafford, like most of us, wants the best of two impossible worlds.

Wanting the best of both East and West, Jean Stafford cannot live comfortably in either. She attempts to resolve her conflict by discarding the worst and keeping the best of the two worlds. Her fiction reflects this attempt; and consequently, many of her stories show the conflict of the two cultures. Usually East and West clash with a jarring discord, but occasionally the civilized East and the primitive West merge to produce a new culture which surpasses either of the two.

The stories which depict the cultural clash of East and West are not Miss Stafford's best. The central conflict, as in "The Bleeding Heart," is simply between a man and his environment—simply a physical clash.

From "The Noble Wicked West of Jean Stafford," *Western American Literature* 7 (1973): 261–70. Reprinted by permission. (Notes renumbered for clarity.)

But in the stories which unite the best of East and West, as in "The Tea Time of Stouthearted Ladies," Jean Stafford shows the tension of a dramatic conflict in which a man struggles with himself, and in this way Stafford achieves both a philosophic and an artistic success.

The West for Miss Stafford is a place where one has the opportunity for physical and mental catharsis, but it lacks the opportunity for aesthetic development. In the cultural East one can develop aesthetically; however, one may also become artificial and effete. In the West one can perceive directly what is honest and true, but too often the crude West so blunts man's aesthetic spirit that he becomes insensitive to everything except the physical. . . .

Jean Stafford's view of the West was heavily influenced by two books which she read as a child—her father's *When Cattle Kingdom Fell*, and her cousin's *A Stepdaughter of the Prairie*. The conceptions of the West in these two novels reflect not only the immediate background of Miss Stafford's Colorado home, but of America as well. The two views portrayed in these novels are held in the phrase "the golden savage land,"[3] or to use Miss Stafford's terms, "the noble wicked West."

For centuries, from Horace to Horace Greeley, men have looked hopefully to the west, futilely searching for the golden land, hoping someone will point and say, as Shakespeare said in *Twelfth Night*, "There lies your way, due west. / Then Westward-hoe. . . ."

In contrast to the golden view is the view of William Bradford who saw the New World to the West as a hideous wilderness which must be subdued. But Shakespeare looked beyond the narrow view of his countrymen, and also beyond the views of men who came much later. In *The Tempest* Shakespeare satirized both the savage and the golden views. He affirmed, as Leo Marx has said "an intellectual and humanistic ideal of high civilization,"[4] believing that only through humanistic love and civilized skills could a liveable world be made out of the land which lay "due west."

James Fenimore Cooper, two hundred years later, carried on this intellectual, humanistic tradition in America. Henry Nash Smith has pointed out that the character of Leatherstocking was originally "conceived in terms of the antithesis between nature and civilization, between freedom and law, that has governed most American interpretations of the westward movement."[5] Cooper, like Jean Stafford one hundred and fifty years later, had a conflict of interest between the freedom and independence of the natural man and the laws and social responsibilities of the civilized man. "The profundity,"

Smith notes, and part of the failure "of the symbol of Leatherstocking springs from the fact that Cooper displays a genuine ambivalence toward all these issues, although in every case his strongest commitment is to the forces of order."[6]

Like Cooper, Jean Stafford portrays in her fiction an attitude toward the West which shows the strong influence of the mixture of the golden-savage views, and like Shakespeare and Cooper, civilization is never discarded for a primitive landscape. But unlike Cooper, Jean Stafford attempts to reconcile her ambivalent attitudes about East and West. And different from Shakespeare, Stafford's civilization is *in* the West— an easternized West, not a westernized East. The civilized East must come to the setting of the primitive West; the trappings of civilization are portable, but the landscape of the West isn't. Shakespeare's Prospero returns to the Old World; but in America, Leatherstocking must die with his socks on somewhere out there on the prairie.

Notes

1. Nina B. Baker, "Jean Stafford," *Wilson Library Bulletin*, XXV (April 1951), 578.

2. *Ibid.*

3. Jack H. Adamson, *The Golden Savage Land* (Salt Lake City: University of Utah, 1967).

4. Leo Marx, *The Machine in the Garden* (New York: Oxford University Press, 1968), p. 57.

5. Henry Nash Smith, *Virgin Land* (New York: Alfred A. Knopf, Inc., 1950), p. 66.

6. *Ibid.*, p. 68.

Melody Graulich

Of the few critics who have written about Jean Stafford, a Pulitzer Prize winner in 1970, most begin their essays, as I do, with a comment about the lack of critical attention her fine work has received.[1] This neglect seems especially surprising among feminists, for much of Stafford's fiction explores the consequences of rigid sex roles. In her three novels, *Boston Adventure* (1944), *The Mountain Lion* (1947), and *The Catherine Wheel* (1952), and in some of her best stories, she shows the price women pay for wearing enforced social masks which deface their inner selves. Pressured to be attentive ("Beatrice Trueblood's Story"), proper ("Polite Conversation"), thin ("The Echo and the Nemesis"), and beautiful ("The End of a Career"), Stafford's women rebel only indirectly, and often self-destructively. Although their needs for authority and a measure of free will cause the fictions' conflicts, these heroines are often too self-effaced to assert a self apart from social norms. They assent to their prescribed identities because they can find no social space for their real selves, which they nurture in a private world of alienation Stafford called "The Interior Castle."

While Stafford's women have learned to conform, her girls hold on as long as they can to their rebellion. Two of these adolescent rebels, Molly Fawcett, the heroine of the critically neglected *The Mountain Lion*, and Emily Vanderpool, the narrator of the title story in *Bad Characters* (1964), struggle to escape from conventional definitions of masculine and feminine behavior so powerful that they cannot be challenged without consequences. While Molly's refusal to conform leads to her violent death, Emily "grows up" by compromising her sense of self. In these two stories, Stafford suggests that girls cannot escape stereotyped women's roles, that the young female rebel should give up on the possibility of becoming Huckleberry Finn and accept that she must be an Elsie Dinsmore.[2]

From "Jean Stafford's Western Childhood: Huck Finn Joins the Camp Fire Girls," *Denver Quarterly*, Vol. 18, No. 1 (Spring 1983): 39–55. Reprinted by permission. (Notes renumbered for clarity.)

Molly and Emily, Stafford has hinted, possess much of her own childhood character.[3] Like their creator, the two girls are raised in the West, the setting for the masculine themes of escape and rebellion which have dominated the American literary canon from Cooper to Fiedler, where masculinity and femininity have become so stripped down and antithetical that they are reduced, depending on one's point of view, to myths or to clichés: the never-changing book jacket image of the freedom-loving, identity-seeking man and his sidekick leaving behind the fences, houses, and churches of the dogma-spouting, civilizing woman. Stafford makes the West a major theme in both fictions in order to explore the pressures of growing up in a world dominated by such myths, and her stories' autobiographical nature helps illuminate her struggles as a woman writer using male conventions and writing within a male tradition. . . .

Many women writers, too, have characterized themselves as representatives of the social world, but they present themselves as protagonists, not antagonists, as constructors and not destroyers. Stafford's cousin Margaret lived the myth of the "noble West," where, in sharp contrast to the male archetype based on freedom from social contract, the writer values pioneer cooperation and women's contribution to building community. While the journals of the first women to go west frequently express a longing for the East, for the networks they left behind, "as the period of isolation came to an end, women's social contacts multiplied. . . . With growth came the opportunity to carry out the civilizing mission.[4] In nostalgic and cheerful accounts, the "stepdaughters of the prairie" stress the powerful role women played in breaking the isolation their mothers had found so difficult to bear, in creating a culture based on their understanding of humanity's needs for communication, manners, and art. Although she may be high-spirited, brave, and even independent, the noble western woman is nevertheless a "joiner" who supports institutions and subdues in herself any anti-social western spirit.[5]

By emphasizing in her preface that she is not a "regional writer," but that her roots remain in the West, Stafford seems to imply that while her fiction may not always be *about* the West, it is *of* the West, the area that shaped her fundamental attitudes toward the self and its relations to the world around it. Her ironic focus on the tension between the wicked and the noble Wests suggests, despite her comic disclaimer, that she saw the interplay between these two myths as a significant influence on the western character. Through her creation of Molly and

Emily, she questions the rebellious-male-and-civilizing-female stereo-
types and shows their effect on a woman's developing sense of her
own capacities and her place in the world.

Notes

1. I refer within the text to those few articles which influenced my reading
of Stafford, but interested readers might also look at Olga W. Vickery, "The
Novels of Jean Stafford," *Critique*, 5 (1962), 14–26; "Jean Stafford and the
Ironic Vision," *South Atlantic Quarterly*, 61 (Autumn, 1962), 484–91; Stuart L.
Burns, "Counterpoint in Jean Stafford's *The Mountain Lion*," *Critique*, 9 (1967),
20–32; and Sidney L. Jenson, "The Noble Wicked West of Jean Stafford,"
Western American Literature, 7 (Winter, 1973), 261–70. Despite Jenson's title,
our essays have little in common because he does not consider the effect of
gender on Stafford's characters, an issue largely ignored in Stafford criticism.
I have not had to argue against these earlier critics because my colleague
Barbara White, whose insights have affected my own reading, has already done
so in a fine essay, "Initiation, the West, and the Hunt in Jean Stafford's *The
Mountain Lion*," forthcoming in *Essays in Literature*.

2. Elsie Dinsmore is the child heroine of a series of pious books for little
girls, written by Martha Farquharson Finley (1828–1909). Molly calls her sisters
"Elsie Dinsmores."

3. See the Authors' Notes to *Bad Characters* (New York: Farrar, Straus,
and Giroux, 1964), and *The Mountain Lion* (Albuquerque: University of New
Mexico Press, 1972), xvii–xix.

4. Julie Roy Jeffrey, *Frontier Women: The Trans-Mississippi West, 1840–80*
(New York: Hill & Wang, 1979), p. 79.

5. Feminist critics are still arguing about whether "liberation" is a major
theme in the writing of western women. For a good summary, see Susan
Armitage, "Western Women's History: A Review Essay," *Frontiers: A Journal
of Women's Studies*, 5 (Fall, 1980), 71–73. I am dealing here not with historical
reality but with myth; probably few men, despite Turner's thesis, lived the
male myth.

Joyce Carol Oates

Certainly the stories are exquisitely wrought, sensitively imagined: like glass flowers, or arabesques, or the "interior castle" of Pansy Vanneman's brain ("Not only the brain as the seat of consciousness, but the physical organ itself which she envisioned, romantically, now as a jewel, now as a flower, now as a light in a glass, now as an envelope of rosy vellum containing other envelopes, one within the other, diminishing infinitely"). Dramatic tension is subdued, in a sense forced underground, so that while narrative conflict between individuals is rare, an extraordinary pressure is built up within the protagonists, who appear trapped inside their own heads, inside their lives (or the social roles their "lives" have become), and despair of striking free. Intelligence and self-consciousness and even a measure of audacity are not quite enough to assure freedom, as the heroines of the late stories "Beatrice Trueblood's Story" and "The End of a Career" discover painfully; even "the liberation" of Polly Bay (in the story with that title) will strike the sympathetic reader as desperate, an adolescent's gesture. The finest of Jean Stafford's stories possess an eerily elegiac tone, though they are never morbid or self-pitying. "In the Zoo" tells a frightful tale, the narrator confesses that "my pain becomes intolerable," but the story concludes with an extravagant outburst of paranoia that manages to be comic as well as distressing; and poor Ramona/Martha Dunn of the early story "The Echo and the Nemesis," trapped within layers of fat, achieves a sort of grotesque triumph over the "normal" and unimaginative Sue, who can only flee in terror the spirited (and insatiable) appetite Ramona represents. ("I am exceptionally ill," Ramona tells her friend, with as much pride as if she were saying, "I am exceptionally talented" or "I am exceptionally attractive.")

This is an art that curves inward toward the meditative, the reminiscent, given life not by bold gestures or strokes but by a patient accumu-

From "The Interior Castle: The Art of Jean Stafford's Short Fiction," *Shenandoah* 30 (Winter 1979): 61–64. Reprinted from *Shenandoah*: The Washington and Lee University Review, with the permission of the Editor.

lation of sharply-observed impressions: the wealth of a poet's eye, or a painter's. "The Lippia Lawn," for instance, is an exercise in recollection, so graphically presented as to allow the reader to share in the young woman's grasping, groping effort to isolate an image out of her past. The "friendless old bachelor" Mr. Oliphant, while an arresting character in himself, is far less real than the protagonist's thoughts—the "interior castle" of her subjectivity. She half-listens to the old man's chatter as "the tenuous memory wove in and out of my thoughts, always tantalizingly just ahead of me. Like the butterfly whose yellow wings are camouflaged to look like sunlight, the flower I could not remember masqueraded as arbutus. . . . Slowly, like a shadow, the past seeped back. A wise scout was reconnoitering for me and at last led me to a place where I never would have looked." In the deceptively tranquil, slow-moving "A Country Love Story" the young wife May eludes her husband Daniel—the tyranny of his almost reasonable madness—by imagining for herself a lover, a lover whose natural place is in an antique sleigh in the front yard of their home. The lover possesses a ghostly plausibility: ". . . there was a delicate pallor on his high, intelligent forehead and there was an invalid's langour in his whole attitude. He wore a white blazer and gray flannels and there was a yellow rosebud in his lapel. Young as he was, he did not, even so, seem to belong to her generation; rather, he seemed to be the reincarnation of someone's uncle as he had been fifty years before." Escaping the oppressive authority of her cerebral husband, May drifts into a sinister, because more seductive and satisfying predicament; by the story's end she and Daniel have traded places. ("A Country Love Story" bears an interesting relationship to a very late story of Jean Stafford's, "Lives of the Poets," [sic] published in 1978.)

One cannot quarrel with the prevailing critical assessment that finds Jean Stafford's art "poised," "highly reflective," "fastidious," "feminine." And certainly she worked within the dominant fictional mode or consciousness of her time—there are no experimental tales in the *Collected Stories* (which cover the years 1944–1969); no explorations beyond the Jamesian-Chekhovian-Joycean model in which most "literary" writers wrote during those years. (Joycean, that is, in terms of *Dubliners* alone.) Each story remains within the consciousness of an intelligent and highly sensitive observer who assembles details from the present and summons forth details from the past, usually with a graceful, urbane irony; each story moves toward an "epiphany," usually in the very last sentence. There is very little that remains mysterious in Stafford's stories, little that is perplexing or disturbing in terms of technique, structure, or style. Some of the stories, it must be admitted, are marred by an arch, over-written self-consciousness, too elaborate, too artificial, to have arisen naturally from the fable at hand (as in "I Love Someone," "Children Are Bored on Sunday," "The Captain's Gift"). Characters tend to resemble one another in speech and manners, and there is little distinction between men and women; occasionally the author offers clichés in place of careful observation—Beatrice Trueblood's neighborhood in New York City, for instance, is quickly assembled along the lines of a stage setting: there are rowdy street urchins, a bloody-faced "bum" on the sidewalk, brick facades of "odious mustardy brown."

When one considers the finest of the stories, however, one is impressed by the rigorous structure that underlies the "beautiful" prose. And there are of course sudden jarring images, sudden reversals, that brilliantly challenge the sensibility evoked by the fiction's near-constant authorial voice—which is, for the most part, reflective, obsessively analytical, compulsively self-conscious. Consider the brutal yet light-hearted—and charming!—Dr. Reinmuth of "The Maiden," offering as a dinnertable anecdote in post-war Heidelberg the story of how, invigorated by a guillotining he saw at the age of twenty-three, he rushed to propose to his presumably genteel German sweetheart. (Astonishing his fellow guests with his recollection of the guillotining Dr. Reinmuth says zestfully: "One, he was horizontal! Two, the blade descended! Three, the head was off the carcass and the blood shot out from the neck like a volcano, a geyser, the flame from an explosion. . . . I did not faint. You remember that this was a beautiful day in spring? And that I was a young man, all dressed up at seven in the morning? . . . I took the train to Fürth and I called my sweetheart. . . . 'I know it's an unusual time of day to call, but I have something unusual to say. Will you marry me?' ") Consider the vicious killing of Shannon, the monkey, by Gran's "watchdog" (and alter ego) Caesar of "In The Zoo"—and Caesar's protracted death-agonies when, next day, he is poisoned by Shannon's grieving owner. Less dramatic, perhaps, but no less cruel, is the haircut poor little Hannah must endure, as part of the ongoing duel of wife and husband in "Cops and Robbers," one of the most successful of the stories. The most startling image in all of Stafford's fiction is the "perfectly cooked baby"—a black baby, of course—offered to the racist Sundstrom by a similarly racist friend in "A Modest Proposal": "It was charred on the outside, naturally, but

I knew it was bound to be sweet and tender inside. So I took him home . . . and told [Sundstrom] to come along for dinner. I heated the toddler up and put him on a platter and garnished him with parsley . . . and you never saw a tastier dish in your life. . . . And what do you think he did after all the trouble I'd gone to? Refused to eat any of it, the sentimentalist! And *he* called *me* a cannibal!" (It is one of the ironies of "A Modest Proposal" that the reader never learns whether the incident ever happened, or whether the speaker has been telling a tall tale to upset the Captain's guests.)

Subdued and analytical and beautifully-constructed stories, then, in what might be called a "conventional" fictional mode: but they are not to be too quickly grasped, too glibly assessed. The "interior castle" of Stafford's art is one which will repay close scrutiny for its meanings open slowly outward, and each phrase, each word, is deliberately chosen. Consider, for instance, the terrifying yet rigorously controlled conclusion of Pansy Vanneman's parable-like story: "The knives ground and carved and curried and scoured the wounds they made; the scissors clipped hard gristle and the scalpels chipped off bone. It was as if a tangle of tiny nerves were being cut dexterously, one by one; the pain writhed spirally and came to her who was a pink bird and sat on the top of a cone. The pain was a pyramid made of a diamond; it was an intense light; it was the hottest fire, the coldest chill, the highest peak, the fastest force, the furthest reach, the newest time. It possessed nothing of her but its one infinitesimal scene: beyond the screen as thin as gossamer, the brain trembled for its life. . . ." After the operation Pansy knows herself violated, her interior castle plundered; she is both healing, and doomed. She lies unmoving "as if in a hammock in a pause of bitterness. She closed her eyes, shutting herself up within her treasureless head."

Philip Stevick

I begin with a passage obviously intended to be dense, rich, and evocative, carefully made, self-conscious, but solidly of the late modernist period, unmistakably *before* the work of the postrealist, postmodernist writers who are my subject. Jean Stafford's "A Country Love Story" begins in this way:

> An antique sleigh stood in the yard, snow after snow banked up against its eroded runners. Here and there upon the bleached and splintery seat were wisps of horsehair and scraps of the black leather that had once upholstered it. It bore, with all its jovial curves, an air not so much of desuetude as of slowed-down dash, as if weary horses, unable to go another step, had at last stopped here. The sleigh had come with the house. The former owner, a gifted businesswoman from Castine who bought old houses and sold them again with all their pitfalls still intact, had said when she was showing them the place, "A picturesque detail, I think," and, waving it away, had turned to the well, which, with enthusiasm and at considerable length, she had said had never gone dry. Actually, May and Daniel had found the detail more distracting than picturesque, so nearly kin was it to outdoor arts and crafts.[1]

The most conspicuous feature of the passage, if one is thinking of obvious contrasts with the experimental fiction of our own decade, is the treatment of time and physical objects. "An antique sleigh," "snow after snow," "eroded runners," phrases like these from the first sentence begin to present a durational mode that is little short of obsessive, projecting us immediately into a world of waiting, expecting, contemplating, appreciating, hoping, wondering, all of those experiences in which the mind and the sensibility are deployed around the central object of the contemplation, slow change. Both objects and people bear with them the marks of their own past; everything decays and

From *Alternative Pleasures: Postrealist Fiction and the Tradition* (Urbana: University Press of Illinois, 1981). © 1981 by the Board of Trustees of the University of Illinois.

disintegrates; both nature and people present the appearance of cyclic or ritualistically recurring behavior. In addition, time, in that passage and in such fiction in general, always carries with it an implicit valuation. A character shows his age gracefully or clumsily; the process of aging carries with it great dignity or great pathos; an aging object carries with it a sense of decreased value, as a result of its diminished usefulness, or a sense of enhanced value, as a result of its tasteful durability. And so it is that we are unsure, in that first paragraph, whether the sleigh is worn out, and should be discarded, or is an authentic antique, and should be preserved. There is no doubt that the cyclic, ritualistic house-buying and -selling of the "gifted business-woman" is specious and faintly repulsive.

It need hardly be said that no one goes through life with his eye so firmly fixed on the clock as this, saying to himself, A is older than B, but B bears its age more gracefully than A. Such an obsession with time is a convention which we never particularly noticed as a convention when a great deal of fiction was written in that way. Yet, stylized and conventionalized though it may have been, such an obsession with time in modernist fiction surely represents a mode of perceiving the world and feeling its rhythms, shared, in a more diffuse and less specialized way, by the general culture.

Furthermore, Jean Stafford's paragraph evokes a set of relationships between two different modes of existence, in this case the man-made object and the forces of the natural world, and these relationships are played upon in a symbolic way. The function of a sleigh is to ride in the snow, not to be covered by it. And we know, even from the first sentence, that the presence of the sleigh, immobile and nonfunctional, will be made into a metaphor, charged with a flexible, ironic value, a metaphor for the presence of man in the world. As in the case of time, such a man-nature dichotomy, as a center for a symbolic charge of meaning, is a convention, present in the kind of sensibility fiction that Jean Stafford represents. In fact, it is a device central to innumerable novelists in the nineteenth century, such as the Brontës, Dickens, and Hardy. A Romantic way of focusing one's consciousness of the world, that man-nature dichotomy is a familiar device both of fiction and the general culture for a hundred years.

Moreover, there is, in Jean Stafford's story, the presence of the thing itself, an object pulled out of the background and conspicuously placed before our attention, described from a double viewpoint, near and far, given a touch of the pathetic fallacy (the sleigh has "jovial curves"), and above all invested with taste. The sleigh, of course, is a chameleon image and is in good taste or bad according to its human context. And it is a marvelously versatile structural device, which compresses and gathers together a number of attitudes axial to the story that follows. But there is not much doubt that the image of the sleigh is more than a trope or a structural device to Jean Stafford and her readers. It is a *thing*, with intricacy of contour, complexity of texture, solidity, and the marks of its own past. Whatever its usefulness in the story, it is an image that issues from the imagination of a writer fascinated with the material objects of daily, sensory existence, a mode of understanding central to Anglo-American fiction from Defoe to what survives of the realistic tradition in the present time.

Note

1. *The Collected Stories* (New York: Farrar, Straus & Giroux, 1969), p. 133.

Maureen Ryan

If the facts of her life exerted an influence on Stafford's work, the era in which she grew up was significant as well. Jean Stafford, born during the war whose end brought the beginning of the twentieth century and the "modern" period, was—almost inevitably—a modernist. As "Souvenirs of Survival" and many of her stories demonstrate, Stafford was keenly aware of the poverty and injustice of the Great Depression. Her fiction exhibits, too, the pervasive influence of World War II on modern society. The terrors of the war hover in the background of "The Maiden," "The Captain's Gift," "The Home Front," and other stories, and war-inspired nihilism and loss of faith in human ideals reverberate throughout her stories. Unable to believe in the possibility of positive change, Stafford and her contemporaries rejected social action and embraced an art whose value lay in craftsmanship and a conservative regard for tradition. And yet, Stafford the ironist always accepted the validity of ostensibly opposite concepts, and in "The Psychological Novel," her asseveration against social novels, she qualified her rejection of "do-good books" in the statement that best presents her bleak vision of modern society.

Against the backdrop of the violence and chaos of World War II, Stafford explores the accompanying social and cultural dissolution; the questioning of liberal, humanistic ideals; the collapse of the family; the alienated individual's search for self and for communion with others, and dangerously, the alternative retreat into what Stafford calls the "interior castle" of the mind. For Stafford, as for many of her contemporaries, the complexities and horrors of the modern human condition dictated the distanced, objective stance of the ironist. Only thus removed could she present the twentieth-century human situation, the "one great incongruity, the appearance of self-valued and subjectively free but temporally finite egos in a universe that seems to be

From *Innocence and Estrangement in the Fiction of Jean Stafford* by Maureen Ryan. Copyright © 1987 by Louisiana State University Press. Used with permission. (Notes renumbered for clarity.)

utterly alien, utterly purposeless, completely deterministic, and incomprehensibly vast."[1]

Stafford's ironic vision, though a particularly appropriate response to the modern condition, was reinforced by her inheritance of the American literary tradition. American literature has from its beginnings been characterized by antithetical impulses, the innocence and naïve faith in a brave new world shadowed by the dark symbolism of the Puritan tradition. As Richard Chase illustrates, contradictions and dualities are endemic to American literature, so that as Alfred Kazin notes, by Stafford's era, "the greatest single fact about our modern American writing [was] our writers' absorption in every last detail of their American world together with their deep and subtle alienation from it."[2] Stafford inherited and merged in her work the Gothic symbolic tradition of Nathaniel Hawthorne and Herman Melville; the social criticism and novel of manners of Henry James and Edith Wharton; and the comic frontier tradition of Mark Twain and the early local colorists. Her successful manipulation of the paradoxically varied yet similar strains in American literature lends to her work a diversity and vivacity that qualify her as an important minor American writer.

Ultimately, Stafford's modernist sensibility and her American heritage are mediated by a more fundamental birthright; Stafford the ironist and Stafford the American are tempered always by Stafford the woman. If, as Judith Fetterley maintains, in a patriarchal society, "bereft, disinherited, cast out, woman is the Other, the Outsider, a mourner among children," Stafford's affinity for the lost and lonely is the peculiar sympathy of one sufferer for another, a "painful communion," a "honeymoon of cripples," a "nuptial consummation of the abandoned" (*CS*, 381).[3] And, I would argue, her special sympathy for the sufferers in her culture derives from her sex. . . .

Certainly Stafford's characters' ailments, both physical and mental, are metaphors for the modern human being's alienation from society. Yet the theme is particularly appropriate for Stafford's cast of female characters. Social scientists and historians have in recent years examined the relationship between women's position in our society and the prevalence of certain types of illness among women. Eating disorders like anorexia and bulimia; agoraphobia and claustrophobia; aphasia and amnesia; rheumatoid arthritis, and other emotion-affected diseases are particularly common among women. And, as Gilbert and Gubar note, there is in literature a long tradition of delineation of the collateral themes of women and illness. In their analysis of the complementary images in literature of woman as angel and monster, they assert that "it is debilitating to be any woman in a society where women are warned that if they do not behave like angels they must be monsters." A young woman, observe Gilbert and Gubar, "is likely to experience her education in docility, submissiveness, self-lessness as in some ways sickening. To be trained in renunciation is almost necessarily to be trained in ill health, since the human animal's first and strongest urge is to his/her *own* survival, pleasure, assertion."[4] Jean Stafford, herself a notorious hypochondriac who nonetheless genuinely suffered from a variety of illnesses throughout her adulthood, examines the typically feminine escape into illness from the anxieties of life. . . .

As her novels and stories indicate, in technique as well as theme, Jean Stafford is interested in discovery, in the revelatory moment, in the burgeoning of awareness. Appropriately, of all her characters, her children most vividly and cogently present her world view. Handicapped by their youthful inefficacy and their limited knowledge and understanding, these young people are frequently put further at a disadvantage by less common circumstances: some are orphaned and unwanted; some (like Molly Fawcett) are precocious and misunderstood; and nearly all bear the double burden of being both young and female. As the titles of some of her stories about adult female protagonists indicate ("Children Are Bored on Sunday," "The Children's Game"), Stafford metaphorically associates women and children, who, as minority members of a male-dominated society, often share the bleak recognition that life is inequitable.

Yet, despite the intrinsic affinity between women and children in Stafford's world, ironically, her female protagonists rarely have children of their own. Angelica Early, Mary Heath, Cora Maybank, Mary Rand, Beatrice Trueblood, and May in "A Country Love Story" are all married and of childbearing age, but childless, and seem neither to consider having children nor to regret not having them. Perhaps it is because she herself (by necessity) had no children that Stafford did not attempt to recreate the experience of motherhood in her fiction. More likely, however, these characters' memories of the trials of childhood, as well as their adult perceptions of life, have made them reluctant to introduce children into this "improbable world." Certainly childhood memories are significant in many of Stafford's stories of adults. . . .

Technically, Stafford pursues the association between women and children throughout the short stories with imagery that highlights their shared estrangement. Those lonely, dependent women whom Abby

Reynolds has joined in "The Children's Game" are described as pitiful children—"waifs" and "orphans" (*CS*, 22). Mrs. Ramsey, in "The Captain's Gift," is, in her ignorance of reality, "like a child, who, dressed in her mother's clothes, is accepted as a grown-up," and finally, like Molly, and like all other children, even this "innocent child of seventy-five" must grow up (*CS*, 438, 440). Angelica Early is encouraged to preserve her innocence, and is as a result like a child; she has a "girlish" and "innocent" mind, and her eyes have "retained the pale, melting blue of infancy" (*CS*, 449, 450). At the end of her sad career, Angelica welcomes her aunt by holding out her arms "like a child, to be embraced," but rejects the woman's gift of gloves with "infantile fury" (*CS*, 461). And the aunt's pronouncement that "the child had no memories" is for the most part accurate (*CS*, 462). In "A Country Love Story," Daniel is ill and requires special care and consideration as he childishly withdraws from his wife and imagines her guilty actions. Yet, ironically, he continually refers to May as a child. He is described as a "professor catching out a student in a fallacy," and as "a tolerant father" who forgives the ignorant child who is unaware of its transgressions (*CS*, 139, 142). With many other writers, one could simply comment upon the author's perception that women, when they act irrationally, are like children. But Stafford's insight into the complexities and problems of children forbids such a superficial interpretation. For Stafford, women and children, equally powerless and underestimated, share a fundamental alienation from the patriarchal society in which they live.

Thematically, too, Stafford explores the special alliance of women and children. Insentient and indolent, Mrs. Otis in "A Modest Proposal" has passed in the torpid Caribbean heat five of the six weeks that will grant her a divorce. Unamused by her hedonistic host, Captain Sundstrom, whose idea of charm is to entertain his guests with a yarn about "a perfectly cooked baby" that nearly provided the "tastiest dish of his life," Mrs. Otis wanders to the garden with the Captain's binoculars and peers at the beach; "almost at once, as if they had been waiting for her, there appeared . . . a parade of five naked Negro children leading a little horse exactly the color of themselves" (*CS*, 73, 71). She watches the children as they frolic in the water, trying—with eventual success—to ride the horse. A sudden, violent storm erupts, scattering the children and soaking Mrs. Otis, who accepts a towel from the Captain's abused, cringing kitchen boy. Vaguely she associates him with the children on the beach and the roasted baby of the Captain's tall tale: "She observed that he wore a miraculous medal under his open shirt. She looked into his eyes and thought, Angels and ministers of grace defend you. The gaze she met humbled her, for its sagacious patience showed that he knew his amulet protected him against an improbable world. His was all the sufferance and suffering of little children. In his ambiguous tribulation, he sympathized with her, and with great dignity he received the towel, heavy with rain, when she had dried herself" (*CS*, 74). The transcendent moment of recognition and sympathy that Mrs. Otis and the native boy experience is a rapprochement that only kindred souls could share.

Notes

1. D. C. Muecke, *Irony* (London, 1970), 68.

2. Richard L. Chase, *The American Novel and Its Tradition* (New York, 1957), 6–7; Alfred Kazin, *On Native Grounds: An Interpretation of Modern American Prose Literature* (1942); rpr. New York, 1970), ix.

3. Judith Fetterley, *The Resisting Reader: A Feminist Approach to American Fiction* (Bloomington, Ind., 1978), ix.

4. Gilbert and Gubar, *Madwoman in the Attic* (New Haven: Yale University Press, 1979), 54.

Bruce Bawer

Stafford continued to write short stories well into the mid-Sixties. Indeed, as her novels faded in the reading public's memory, she began to be known primarily for her work in that field, and, in particular, as one of the most celebrated practitioners of the controversial genre known as the *New Yorker* story. Stafford's short fiction, most of which was assembled in various volumes during the Fifties and Sixties and brought together in the Pulitzer Prize–winning *Collected Stories* (1969), represents one of the finest moments of the American short story. Witty, luminous, and impeccably crafted, her contributions to the genre are crowded with people named Otis and Meriwether and Fairweather, with troubled children and snobby society women, and with garden-party conversations reported word for word. Extremely long sentences abound, and the vocabulary is unusually rich: a single page of the story "A Modest Proposal" contains the words *concupiscently*, *nares*, *sybarite*, *mufti*, and *cereus*. Yet Stafford succeeds in fashioning a lucid, well-upholstered style into which such words fit very gracefully.

To read *The Collected Stories* is to note the recurrence of certain themes, many of which recall the preoccupations of Stafford's life as well as the plots of her novels. The book abounds in protagonists who are, to some extent, Sonie Marburgs—unsatisfied with their lot and eager to be taken into someone else's world. In "The Bleeding Heart," for instance, "a Mexican girl from the West" named Rose Fabrizio longs to be adopted by a mysterious elderly man who visits the New England library where she works; but her illusions about the man are soon shattered. The most prominent of Stafford's themes, indeed, may well be the shattering of illusions—the illusions of Americans about Europe, of Westerners about the Eastern seaboard, of poor people about the rich, of naïve young people about the *beau monde*. One story after another seems to derive in some way from the young Stafford's encounter with Lucy Cooke's bohemia, with the *Kultur* of Heidelberg,

From "Jean Stafford's Triumph," *New Criterion* 7 (November 1988): 61–72. Reprinted by permission of the author.

Peter Taylor

When one settles down to read Jean Stafford's novels and stories one advisedly has a dictionary—a big dictionary—close by. For she was a literary artist in the most literal sense. Her most profound and her wittiest effects alike are got through words, themselves. And her remarkable diction, her complicated syntax, her elaborate sentence structure all spilled over into her conversation (if it wasn't, as a matter of fact, the other way round) and were to some degree responsible for making her conversation the delight it was. In life—as a conversationalist, that is—she sometimes seemed at once the most articulate and the most inarticulate person one can imagine. She seemed to talk, as she sometimes seemed to write (in retrospect it is often difficult to distinguish between the two)—seemed to talk or write round and round a subject, dazzling you with her diction; but finally when she stopped (and it was hard to stop her) you realized that somewhere back there in her discourse she had penetrated the tough integument (as she might have put it) and touched the core of truth she had been probing for, had done so without your ever having realized that she had got to the heart of the matter. It was as though she wished always to conceal anything in her narrative so vulgar as mere purposefulness—her narrative spoken or written. Sometimes it was only in retrospect, and long after the conversation or the story was finished, that you saw what she had been saying. And somehow her statement was the more effective because of that.

In life Jean was, in a sense, always playing a role. She had many roles, roles like those in her written fiction—a grande dame, a plain spoken old maid, a country girl from the West, a spoiled rich woman, her diction always changing to fit the role. And sometimes she played the role of a writer, a woman writer. This surely entailed as much play-acting as the other roles. For it no more represented the real Jean than

From "A Commemorative Tribute to Jean Stafford," *Shenandoah* 30 (Autumn 1979): 56–60. Reprinted from *Shenandoah*: The Washington and Lee University Review, with the permission of the Editor.

did those other roles, although many people—allegedly sophisticated people—mistook her play-pretend Manhattan bluestocking for the literary genius who wrote under the name of Jean Stafford. Actually, what she was like when she sat down to write her wondrous novels and stories may be something beyond the comprehension of any of us. In a sense, her literary personality remains her best kept secret. Perhaps it was in that role that she was the most private of private persons, and perhaps, in order to preserve that role, it was necessary for her to have the privacy she was always seeking.

Chronology

1915   Born 1 July in Covina, California, the fourth and youngest child of John Richard and Mary Ethel (McKillop) Stafford.

1921   Moves to Colorado with her family after her father experiences financial losses in the stock market.

1925–1932   Attends University Hill School, Boulder; graduates from State Preparatory School, Boulder.

1932   Summer before entering university, works at dude ranch in Ward, Colorado, as a chambermaid and waitress, an experience she treats in "The Tea Time of Stouthearted Ladies."

1932–1936   Attends University of Colorado, Boulder, majoring in English; her mother takes in boarders to supplement the family income; Stafford models nude for art classes, an experience she recounts in "The Philosophy Lesson"; befriends Lucy McKee.

1935   Suicide of Lucy McKee, an event that haunts Stafford throughout her life; shortly after Lucy's death, Stafford begins taking instruction in Catholicism; her parents move to Oregon.

1936   Receives B.A. and M.A. simultaneously from University of Colorado, Boulder; writes master's thesis titled "Profane and Divine Love in English Literature of the Thirteenth Century," directed by Irene McKeehan.

1936–1937   On fellowship from the German government to study philology at the University of Heidelberg, but rarely attends classes and loses interest in her study of philology; begins writing regularly and decides to devote her life to writing, as advised by McKeehan.

1937   Meets Robert Lowell in August at Boulder Writers' Conference, University of Colorado, where her work (and Lowell's) receives honorable mention.

1937–1938   Instructor, Stephens College, Columbia, Missouri, where she begins work on a satiric novel about progressive education, *Neville*, and on *Autumn Festival*, an account of her Heidelberg experience; her story "Caveat Emptor" is based on her year at Stephens; she is asked to leave by the administration for her failure to fit the Stephens mold.

1938   Enrolls briefly in the Ph.D. program at the University of Iowa but hates academia; moves to Concord, Massachusetts, in December; meets Lowell again over the Christmas holiday and is seriously injured in automobile accident with Lowell at the wheel; undergoes the first of many facial reconstructive surgeries.

1939   First story, "And Lots of Solid Color," published in *American Prefaces* (a University of Iowa publication).

1940   Married 2 April to Robert Lowell at St. Mark's Episcopal Church, New York City.

1940–1941   After Lowell's graduation from Kenyon, Stafford and Lowell live in Baton Rouge, where she is a secretary for *Southern Review* and Lowell is a graduate student at Louisiana State University; Lowell converts to Catholicism and insists they be remarried in the Catholic church.

1941–1942   Stafford and Lowell move to New York, where they work for Sheed & Ward, a Catholic publishing house.

1942–1943   Stafford and Lowell live in Monteagle, Tennessee, with Allen Tate and his wife, Caroline Gordon, while Stafford works on her first novel, *Boston Adventure*.

1943   Continues work on *Boston Adventure* at Yaddo Writers Colony, Sarasota Springs, New York.

1944   *Boston Adventure* published by Harcourt Brace, "The Darkening Moon" published in *Harper's Bazaar* (January), "The Lippia Lawn" published under the name Phoebe Lowell in *Kenyon Review* (spring), and "A Reunion" published in *Partisan Review* (fall); receives *Mademoiselle*'s merit award as one of its "10 Women of the Year"; Stafford's brother Dick dies in France, a war casualty.

1945   Awarded Guggenheim fellowship and National Institute of Arts and Letters grant; lecturer at Queens College (now Queens College of the City University of New York); "The Home Front" published in *Partisan Review* (spring) and "Between the Porch and the Altar" published in *Harper's* (June); buys house in Damariscotta Mills, Maine, with proceeds from *Boston Adventure*.

1946   Separates from Robert Lowell; subsequently hospitalized in Payne-Whitney clinic, New York; publishes "The Captain's Gift" in *Sewanee Review* (April) and "The Interior Castle" in *Partisan Review* (November–December).

1947   "The Hope Chest" appears in *Harper's* (January) and "A Slight Maneuver" in *Mademoiselle* (February); *The Mountain Lion*, her second novel, is published by Harcourt Brace; Stafford's mother dies in Oregon; Stafford released from Payne-Whitney in June.

1948   Divorces Robert Lowell; receives Guggenheim fellowship and National Press Club Award; publishes "The Psychological Novel" in *Kenyon Review* (spring) and "Children Are Bored on Sunday," her first *New Yorker* story, in February; "The Bleeding Heart" appears in *Partisan Review* (September) and "A Summer Day" in *New Yorker* (September).

1949   Travels to Europe on assignment for *New Yorker*; publishes in *New Yorker* "The Cavalier" (February), "A Modest Proposal" (July), and "Polite Conversation" (August).

1950   Marries Oliver Jensen, a writer for *Life* magazine, on 28 January in the chapel of Christ Church, New York; Stafford delivers the Sophie Hart Lecture, Wellesley College, Wellesley, Massachusetts, in April (the lecture serves as material for two subsequent articles, "Truth and the Novelist" and "Truth in Fiction"); publishes in *New Yorker* "A Country Love Story" (May), "The Maiden" (July), and "The Echo and the Nemesis" (December) and in *Harper's Bazaar* "Old Flaming Youth" (December).

1951   Publishes "The Healthiest Girl in Town" in *New Yorker* (April) and "Truth and the Novelist" in *Harper's Bazaar* (August).

1952   Publishes her third novel, *The Catherine Wheel*, with Harcourt, Brace; delivers address titled "An Etiquette for Writers" at the 1952 Writers' Conference in the Rocky Mountains, University of Colorado, Boulder; publishes "The Violet Rock" *in New Yorker* (April), "Life Is No Abyss" in *Sewanee Review* (July), "I Love Someone" in *Colorado Quarterly* (summer), and "The Connoisseurs" in *Harper's Bazaar* (October).

1953　Publishes her first collection of short stories, *Children Are Bored on Sunday*, with Harcourt Brace and Random House and another collection, *The Interior Castle* (containing *Boston Adventure*, *The Mountain Lion*, and *Children Are Bored on Sunday*); "In the Zoo" published in the *New Yorker* (September); divorces Oliver Jensen.

1954　Publishes *A Winter's Tale* with Ballantine in *New Short Novels* (with Elizabeth Etnier, Shelby Foote, and Clyde Miller), "Bad Characters" in *New Yorker* (December), and "New England Winter" in *Holiday* (February).

1955　Receives O. Henry Memorial Award for "In the Zoo"; in *New Yorker* publishes "Beatrice Trueblood's Story" (February), "Maggie Meriwether's Rich Experience" (June), and "The Warlock" (December).

1956　Meets A. J. Liebling in London; awarded the Norlin Medal, University of Colorado, Boulder, given to an outstanding graduate of the university; publishes *Stories* with Farrar, Straus, and Cudahy (with John Cheever, Daniel Fuchs, and William Maxwell), "The End of a Career" in *New Yorker* (January), "Caveat Emptor" in *Mademoiselle* (May), "A Reading Problem" in *New Yorker* (June), and "The Mountain Day" in *New Yorker* (August); in summer returns to Heidelberg for a visit.

1957　Publishes in *New Yorker* "My Blithe, Sad Bird" (April) and "A Reasonable Facsimile" (August).

1958　Publishes "The Children's Game" in *Saturday Evening Post* (October).

1959　Marries A. J. Liebling on 3 April in New York; publishes "The Scarlet Letter" in *Mademoiselle* (July).

1960　Publishes "Souvenirs of Survival: The Thirties Revisited" in *Mademoiselle* (February).

1961   Katharine White retires as fiction editor of *New Yorker*.

1962   Stafford publishes two children's books, *The Lion and the Carpenter* with Macmillan and *Elephi: The Cat with the High I.Q.* with Farrar, Straus and Cudahy; serves on the jury for National Book Award in fiction.

1963   Travels to Europe with Liebling; Liebling dies 21 December.

1964   Publishes *Bad Characters* with Farrar, Straus and Co., her third collection of short stories; "The Ordeal of Conrad Pardee" appears in *Ladies' Home Journal* (July) and "The Tea Time of Stouthearted Ladies" in *Kenyon Review* (winter); begins publishing book reviews for *Vogue*.

1964–1965   Fellow at the Center for Advanced Studies, Wesleyan University, Middletown, Connecticut.

1965   Awarded Rockefeller Foundation grant.

1966   Stafford's father dies in Oregon; publishes *A Mother in History* with Farrar, Straus and Giroux (a profile of Lee Harvey Oswald's mother), *Selected Stories of Jean Stafford* with New American Library, and in *Library Journal* "Truth in Fiction" (October).

1967–1973   Adjunct professor at Columbia University, New York.

1968   Publishes "The Philosophy Lesson" in *New Yorker* (November).

1969   Publishes *The Collected Stories*; awarded Ingram-Merrill and Chapelbrook grants.

1970   Awarded Pulitzer Prize in fiction for *Collected Stories*; elected to membership in National Academy of Arts and Letters; is writer-in-residence at Wesleyan University; begins five-year stint writing reviews of children's books for *New Yorker*.

1971   Delivers Barnard Lectures, Barnard College, New York, one of which was later titled "The Felicities of Formal Education."

1972   Awarded Doctor of Humane Letters degree by University of Colorado, Boulder; addresses associates of the Rare Book Room of Norlin Library, University of Colorado,

Boulder (this talk later published as "Miss McKeehan's Pocketbook").

1973 Awarded Litt.D., Southampton College, Long Island; publishes "Men, Women, Language, Science and Other Dichotomies" in *Confrontation* (a Long Island University publication).

1975 Serves on jury for Pulitzer Prize in fiction.

1976 Suffers a stroke, resulting in aphasia.

1977 Robert Lowell dies in New York.

1978 "An Influx of Poets" (extracted by Robert Giroux from Stafford's unfinished novel, *The Parliament of Women*) published in *New Yorker* (November).

1979 Stafford dies 26 March at White Plains, New York; her ashes are placed in Greenriver Cemetery, East Hampton, Long Island, beside the body of A. J. Liebling; "Woden's Day" (extracted by Robert Giroux from *The Parliament of Women*) published in *Shenandoah* (autumn).

Selected Bibliography

Primary Works

Collections of Short Stories

Bad Characters. New York: Farrar, Straus & Giroux, 1964. Includes "Bad
Characters," "The End of a Career," "A Reasonable Facsimile," "In the
Zoo," "Cops and Robbers," "The Liberation," "The Captain's Gift,"
"A Reading Problem," "Caveat Emptor," and *A Winter's Tale*.
Children Are Bored on Sunday. New York: Harcourt, Brace, 1953. Includes "The
Echo and the Nemesis," "A Country Love Story," "A Summer Day,"
"The Maiden," "The Home Front," "Between the Porch and the Altar,"
"The Bleeding Heart," "The Interior Castle," "A Modest Proposal," and
"Children Are Bored on Sunday."
The Collected Stories. New York: Farrar, Straus & Giroux, 1969. Includes *The
Innocents Abroad*: "Maggie Meriwether's Rich Experience," "The Chil-
dren's Game," "The Echo and the Nemesis," "The Maiden," "A Modest
Proposal," and "Caveat Emptor'"; *The Bostonians and Other Manifestations
of the American Scene*: "Life Is No Abyss," "The Hope Chest," "Polite
Conversation," "A Country Love Story," "The Bleeding Heart," "The
Lippia Lawn," and "The Interior Castle"; *Cowboys and Indians, and Magic
Mountains*: "The Healthiest Girl in Town," "The Tea Time of Stout-
hearted Ladies," "The Mountain Day," "The Darkening Moon," "Bad
Characters," "In the Zoo," "The Liberation," "A Reading Problem,"
"A Summer Day," and "The Philosophy Lesson"; *Manhattan Island*:
"Children Are Bored on Sunday," "Beatrice Trueblood's Story," "Be-
tween the Porch and the Altar," "I Love Someone," "Cops and Robbers,"
"The Captain's Gift," and "The End of a Career."
The Interior Castle. New York: Harcourt, Brace, 1953. Includes *Boston Adventure*,
The Mountain Lion, and *Children Are Bored on Sunday*.
Selected Stories of Jean Stafford. New York: New American Library, 1966. In-
cludes "The Echo and the Nemesis," "A Country Love Story," "A Sum-
mer Day," "The Maiden," "The Home Front," "A Modest Proposal,"
"Children Are Bored on Sunday," "Bad Characters," "The End of a
Career," "A Reasonable Facsimile," "Cops and Robbers," "The Libera-
tion," "The Captain's Gift," "Caveat Emptor," *A Winter's Tale*, and "Beatrice Trueblood's Story."

Stories (with John Cheever, Daniel Fuchs, and William Maxwell). New York: Farrar, Straus & Cudahy, 1956. Includes "The Liberation," "In the Zoo," "Bad Characters," "Beatrice Trueblood's Story," and "Maggie Meriwether's Rich Experience."

Uncollected Stories

"And Lots of Solid Color." *American Prefaces* 5 (November 1939): 22–25.
"The Cavalier." *New Yorker*, 12 February 1949, 28–36.
"The Connoisseurs." *Harper's Bazaar*, October 1952, 198, 232, 234, 240, 246.
"An Influx of Poets." *New Yorker*, 6 November 1978, 43–60.
"Mountain Jim." *Boy's Life*, February 1968, 27, 66–67.
"My Blithe, Sad Bird." *New Yorker*, 6 April 1957, 30–38.
"Old Flaming Youth." *Harper's Bazaar*, December 1950, 94, 182–84, 188.
"The Ordeal of Conrad Pardee." *Ladies' Home Journal*, July 1964, 58, 78, 80–83.
"A Reunion." *Partisan Review* 11 (Autumn 1944): 423–27.
"The Scarlet Letter." *Mademoiselle*, July 1959, 62–68, 100–1.
"A Slight Maneuver." *Mademoiselle*, February 1947, 177, 282–87, 289.
"The Violet Rock." *New Yorker*, 26 April 1952, 34–42.
"The Warlock." *New Yorker*, 24 December 1955, 25–28, 30–45.
"Woden's Day." *Shenandoah* 30 (Autumn 1979): 5–26.

Selections from Novels Published as Stories

"Hotel Barstow" (from *Boston Adventure*). *Partisan Review* 11 (Summer 1944): 243–64.
"In the Snowfall" (excerpt from Stafford's unpublished novel *In the Snowfall*, edited by Carolyn Ezell Foster). *South Carolina Review* 24 (Spring 1992): 139–153.
"The Tunnel with No End" (from *The Mountain Lion*). *Harper's Bazaar*, January 1947, 102, 153–56.
"Wedding: Beacon Hill" (from *Boston Adventure*). *Harper's Bazaar*, June 1944, 48–50, 84–94.

Novels

Boston Adventure. New York: Harcourt, Brace, 1944.
The Catherine Wheel. New York: Harcourt, Brace, 1952.
The Mountain Lion. New York: Harcourt, Brace, 1947.

Children's Books

Elephi, the Cat with the High I.Q. Illustrated by Erik Blegvad. New York: Farrar, Straus & Cudahy, 1962.

The Lion and the Carpenter and Other Tales from "The Arabian Nights." Retold and introduced by Jean Stafford. Illustrated by Sandro Nardini. New York: Macmillan, 1962.

Nonfiction

A Mother in History (a profile of Lee Harvey Oswald's mother). New York: Farrar, Straus & Giroux, 1966.

Articles, Letters, and Essays

"The Art of Accepting Oneself." *Vogue*, February 1952, 174–75, 242. Reprinted in *The Arts of Living: From the Pages of "Vogue,"* edited by Ernest Dimnet et al., 54–62. New York: Simon & Schuster, 1954.

"At This Point in Time, TV Is Murdering the English Language." *New York Times*, 15 September 1974, sec. 2, pp. 23, 27.

"Coca-Cola." *Esquire*, December 1975, 96, 178–79.

"Contagious Imbecility." *New York Times Book Review*, 5 May 1974, 8–12.

"The Crossword Puzzle Has Gone to Hell." *Esquire*, December 1974, 144–47.

"Divorce: Journey through Crisis." *Harper's Bazaar*, November 1958, 134–35, 152.

"Don't Send Me Gladiolus." *Vogue*, March 1973, 146.

"Don't Use Ms. with Miss Stafford, unless You Mean ms." *New York Times*, 21 September 1973, 36.

"East Hampton from the Catbird Seat." *New York Times*, 26 December 1971, sec. 1A, pp. 1, 13.

"Enchanted Island." *Mademoiselle*, May 1950, 85, 140–41.

"Heroes and Villains: Who Was Famous and Why." *McCall's*, April 1976, 196–99, 265–67, 270.

"Home for Christmas." *Mademoiselle*, December 1951, 78, 108–10.

"Intimations of Hope." *McCall's*, December 1971, 77, 118, 120.

Introduction to *The American Coast*. New York: Charles Scribner's, 1971, 15–27.

Introduction to *The Press*, by A. J. Liebling, 2nd ed., rev. New York: Ballantine, 1975, ix-xiii.

"Katharine Graham." *Vogue*, December 1973, 202–5, 218–19, 221.

"Letter from Edinburgh." *New Yorker*, 17 September 1949, 83–88.

"Letter from Germany." *New Yorker*, 3 December 1949, 79–91.

"Love among the Rattlesnakes." *McCall's*, March 1970, 69, 145–46.

"Men, Women, Language, Science, and Other Dichotomies." *Confrontation* 7 (Fall 1973): 69–74.

"Miss McKeehan's Pocketbook." *Colorado Quarterly* 24 (Spring 1976): 407–11.

"Millicent Fenwick Makes an Adroit Politician." *Vogue*, June 1975, 120, 139–40.

"Modern Romanticism: Lally Weymouth." *Vogue*, June 1974, 86, 145.

"My Sleep Grew Shy of Me." *Vogue*, October 1947, 135, 171, 174.

"My (Ugh!) Sensitivity Training." *Horizon*, Spring 1970, 112.

"New England Winter." *Holiday*, February 1954, 34–37. Reprinted in *Ten Years of "Holiday,"* 340–47. New York: Simon & Schuster, 1956.

"New York Is a Daisy." *Harper's Bazaar*, December 1958, 73 + .

"On Books to Read before Sleep." *Mademoiselle*, February 1975, 154, 156, 159.

"On My Mind." *Vogue*, November 1973, 200–1, 250, 254.

"The Plight of the American Language" (delivered as Barnard Lecture, Barnard College, 1971, under the title "Carcinoma in the American Language"). *Saturday Review World*, 4 December 1973, 14–18.

"Profiles: An American Town." *New Yorker*, 28 August 1948, 26–37.

"The Psychological Novel." *Kenyon Review* 10 (Spring 1948): 214–27.

"To School with Joy." *Vogue*, May 1968, 258–61, 128.

"Some Advice to Hostesses from a Well-Tempered Guest." *Vogue*, September 1974, 296–98.

"Somebody out There Hates Me." *Esquire*, August 1974, 108–9, 156.

"Some Letters to Peter and Eleanor Taylor." *Shenandoah* 30 (Autumn 1979): 27–55.

"Souvenirs of Survival: The Thirties Revisited." *Mademoiselle*, February 1960, 90–91, 174–76.

"Statement." *Saturday Review*, 6 October 1962, 50.

"The Strange World of Marguerite Oswald." *McCall's*, October 1965, 112–13, 192–94, 196–200, 202.

"Suffering Summer Houseguests." *Vogue*, August 1971, 112.

"Truth in Fiction." *Library Journal* 91 (October 1966): 4557–65.

"Truth and the Novelist." *Harper's Bazaar*, August 1951, 139, 187–89. Reprinted in *Explorations: Reading, Thinking, Discussion, Writing*, edited by Thomas Clark Pollock et al., 169–78. Englewood Cliffs, N.J.: Prentice Hall, 1956.

"The Unexpected Joys of a Simple Garden." *Redbook*, June 1971, 79, 179–80.

"What Does Martha Mitchell Know?" *McCall's*, October 1972, 8–10, 28–31, 120.

"Why I Don't Get around Much Anymore." *Esquire*, March 1975, 114, 132–34.

"Wordman, Spare That Tree!" (delivered at Barnard College, 1971, under the title "Teaching Writing"). *Saturday Review World*, 13 July 1974, 14–17.

"Young Writers." *Analects* 1 (October 1960): 16–24.

Book Reviews

(Jean Stafford wrote more than 100 book reviews during her career; I include here those most relevant to the short story genre and most revealing of Stafford's criteria for judging the fiction of other writers.)

"Empty Net" (a review of *"The Wide Net" and Other Stories*, by Eudora Welty). *Partisan Review* 11 (Winter 1944): 114–15.

Review of *Ada*, by Vladimir Nabokov. *Vogue*, June 1969, 64, 66

Review of *Les Belles Images*, by Simone de Beauvoir. *Vogue*, March 1968, 46.

Review of *In Cold Blood*, by Truman Capote. *Vogue*, January 1966, 35.

Review of *The Day We Got Drunk on Cake*, by William Trevor. *Vogue*, February 1968, 108.

Review of *The Door in the Wall*, by Oliver La Farge. *Vogue*, February 1965, 97.

Review of *My Heart Is Broken*, by Mavis Gallant. *Vogue*, April 1964, 56.

Review of *The Last Gentleman*, by Walker Percy. *Vogue*, August 1966, 58.

Review of *Lost in the Funhouse*, by John Barth. *Vogue*, August 1968, 48.

Review of *A Lost Lady*, by Willa Cather. *Washington [D.C.] Post Book World*, 26 August 1973, 1–3.

Review of *La Maison de Rendez-vous*, by Alain Robbe-Grillet. *Vogue*, January 1967, 52.

Review of *Naked in Garden Hills*, by Harry Crews. *New York Times Book Review*, 13 April 1969, 4–5.

Review of *"The Ragman's Daughter" and Other Stories*, by Alan Sillitoe. *Vogue*, January 1964, 27.

Review of *Signs and Wonders*, by Françoise Mallet-Joris. *Vogue*, August 1967, 74.

Review of *The Soul of Kindness*, by Elizabeth Taylor. *Vogue*, July 1964, 32.

Review of *When She Was Good*, by Philip Roth. *Vogue*, February 1967, 63.

"Sensuous Women" (review of *Kate Chopin: A Critical Biography*, by Per Seyersted, and *The Complete Works of Kate Chopin*, edited by Per Seyersted). *New York Review of Books*, 23 September 1971, 33–35.

Secondary Works

Interviews

Bond, Alice Dixon. "Fascination with Words Started Jean Stafford on Writing Career." *Boston Sunday Herald*, 27 January 1952, n.p.

Breit, Harvey. "Talk with Jean Stafford." *New York Times Book Review*, 20

January 1952, 18. Reprinted in *The Writer Observed*, ed. Harvey Breit 223–25. New York: World Publishing, 1956.

Hutchens, John K. "On an Author." *New York Herald Tribune Book Review*, 24 May 1953, 2.

Whitman, Alden. "Jean Stafford and Her Secretary 'Harvey' Reigning in Hamptons." *New York Times*, 26 August 1973, 104.

Books

Davis, Linda H. *Onward and Upward: A Biography of Katharine S. White*. New York: Fromm International, 1987.

Eisinger, Chester. *Fiction of the Forties*. Chicago: University of Chicago Press, 1963.

Gilbert, Sandra, and Susan Gubar. *The Madwoman in the Attic: The Woman Writer and the Nineteenth-Century Literary Imagination*. New Haven, Conn.: Yale University Press, 1979.

Goodman, Charlotte Margolis. *Jean Stafford: The Savage Heart*. Austin: University of Texas Press, 1990.

Hamilton, Ian. *Robert Lowell: A Biography*. New York: Random House, 1982.

Heller, Dana. *The Feminization of Quest-Romance: Radical Departures*. Austin: University of Texas Press, 1990.

Heymann, C. David. *American Aristocracy*. New York: Dodd, Mead, 1980.

Hulbert, Ann. *The Interior Castle: The Art and Life of Jean Stafford*. New York: Alfred A. Knopf, 1992.

Kolodny, Annette. *The Land before Her*. Chapel Hill: University of North Carolina Press, 1984.

La Belle, Jenijoy. *Herself Beheld: The Literature of the Looking Glass*. Ithaca, N.Y.: Cornell University Press, 1988.

Roberts, David. *Jean Stafford: A Biography*. Boston: Little, Brown, 1988.

Russ, Joanna. *The Heroine's Text*. New York: Columbia University Press, 1980.

Ryan, Maureen. *Innocence and Estrangement in the Fiction of Jean Stafford*. Baton Rouge: Louisiana State University Press, 1987.

Simpson, Eileen. *Poets in Their Youth: A Memoir*. New York: Farrar, Straus & Giroux, 1982.

Sokolov, Raymond. *Wayward Reporter: The Life of A. J. Liebling*. New York: Harper & Row, 1980.

Stevick, Philip. *Alternative Pleasures: Postrealist Fiction and the Tradition*. Urbana: University of Illinois Press, 1981.

Walsh, Mary Ellen Williams. *Jean Stafford*. Boston: Twayne, 1985.

Welty, Eudora. *Place in Fiction*. In *Storytellers and Their Art*, Edited by Georgianne Trask and Charles Burkhart, 236–55. New York: Doubleday, 1963.

Articles and Reviews

Auchincloss, Louis. *Pioneers and Caretakers: A Study of Nine American Women Novelists*. Minneapolis: University of Minnesota Press, 1961. Reprinted by G. K. Hall, 1985.

Bawer, Bruce. "Jean Stafford's Triumph." *New Criterion* 7 (November 1988): 61–72.

Davenport, Guy. "Tough Characters, Solid Novels" (a review of *Bad Characters*). *National Review*, 26 January 1965, 66.

Davidson, Mary V. " 'Defying the Stars and Challenging the Moon': The Early Correspondence of Evelyn Scott and Jean Stafford." *Southern Quarterly* 28 (Summer 1990): 25–34.

Flagg, Nancy. "People to Stay." *Shenandoah* 30 (Autumn 1979): 65–76.

Gerber, John C. *"Tom Sawyer Abroad."* In *The Mark Twain Encyclopedia*, Edited by J. R. LeMaster and James D. Wilson, 739–40. New York: Garland, 1993.

Graulich, Melody. "Jean Stafford's Western Childhood: Huck Finn Joins the Camp Fire Girls." *Denver Quarterly* 18 (Spring 1983): 39–55.

———. " 'O Beautiful for Spacious Guys': An Essay on the 'Legitimate Inclinations of the Sexes.' " In *The Frontier Experience and the American Dream: Essays on American Literature*, edited by David Mogen, Mark Busby, and Paul Bryant, 186–201. College Station: Texas A&M University Press, 1989.

Hassan, Ihab. "Jean Stafford: The Expense of Style and the Scope of Sensibility." *Western Review* 19 (Spring 1955): 185–203.

Janeway, Elizabeth. "The Worlds of Jean Stafford" (a review of *Collected Stories*). *Atlantic*, March 1969, 136–38.

Jenson, Sid. "The Noble Wicked West of Jean Stafford." *Western American Literature* 7 (Winter 1973): 261–70.

Leary, William. "Grafting onto Her Roots: Jean Stafford's 'Woden's Day.' " *Western American Literature* 23 (August 1988): 129–39.

———. "Jean Stafford: The Wound and the Bow." *Sewanee Review* 98 (Summer 1990): 333–49.

———. "Jean Stafford, Katharine White, and the *New Yorker*." *Sewanee Review* 93 (Fall 1985): 584–96.

———. "Native Daughter: Jean Stafford's California." *Western American Literature* 21 (1986): 195–205.

———. "Pictures at an Exhibition: Jean Stafford's 'Children Are Bored on Sunday.' " *Kenyon Review* 49 (Spring 1987): 1–8.

———. "The Suicidal Thirties: Jean Stafford's 'The Philosophy Lesson.' " *Southwest Review* 72 (1987): 389–403.

———. "A Tale of Two Titles: Jean Stafford's 'Caveat Emptor.' " *South Atlantic Quarterly* 85 (Spring 1986): 123–33.

———. "Through Caverns Measureless to Man: Jean Stafford's 'The Interior Castle.' " *Shenandoah* 34 (1983): 79–94.

McConahay, Mary Davidson. " 'Heidelberry Braids' and Yankee *Politesse*: Jean Stafford and Robert Lowell Reconsidered." *Virginia Quarterly Review* 62 (Spring 1986): 213–36.

Mazzaro, Jerome. "Remembrances of Things Proust" (a review of *Bad Characters*). *Shenandoah* 16 (Summer 1965): 114–17.

Moss, Howard. "Jean: Some Fragments." *Shenandoah* 30 (Autumn 1979): 77–84.

Oates, Joyce Carol. "The Interior Castle: The Art of Jean Stafford's Short Fiction." *Shenandoah* 30 (Autumn 1979): 61–64. Reprinted in *The Profane Art: Essays and Reviews*, 123–27. New York: Persea Books, 1985.

Pinkham, Marjorie Stafford. "Jean." *Antaeus* 52 (Spring 1984): 7–32.

Roberts, David. "Jean & Joe: The Stafford-Liebling Marriage." *American Scholar* 57 (Summer 1988): 373–91.

Rosowski, Susan. "The Novel of Awakening." In *The Voyage In: Fictions of Female Development*, 49–68. Edited by Elizabeth Abel, Marianne Hirsch, and Elizabeth Langland. Hanover: University Press of New England, 1983.

Sheed, Wilfred. "Miss Jean Stafford." *Shenandoah* 30 (Autumn 1979): 92–99.

Showalter, Elaine. "Feminist Criticism in the Wilderness." *Critical Inquiry* 8 (Winter 1981): 179–205.

Straus, Dorothea. "Jean Stafford." *Shenandoah* 30 (Autumn 1979): 85–91.

Taylor, Peter. "A Commemorative Tribute to Jean Stafford." *Shenandoah* 30 (Autumn 1979): 56–60.

Twain, Mark. "How to Tell a Story." In *Selected Shorter Works of Mark Twain*, edited by Walter Blair, 239–43. Boston: Houghton Mifflin, 1962.

Vickery, Olga. "Jean Stafford and the Ironic Vision." *South Atlantic Quarterly* 61 (Autumn 1962): 484–91.

Viera, Carroll. " 'In the Zoo' and *The Mill on the Floss*. *American Notes and Queries* 20 (November–December 1981): 53–54.

Wagner, Mary Hegel. A Review of Jean Stafford's *Collected Stories*. *America*, April 1969, 426–27.

Walsh, Mary Ellen Williams. "The Young Girl in the West: Disenchantment in Jean Stafford's Short Fiction." In *Women and Western American Literature*, edited by Helen Winter Stauffer and Susan J. Rosowski, 230–43. Troy, N.Y.: Whitston Publishing, 1982.

Wilson, Mary Ann. "In Another Country: Jean Stafford's Literary Apprenticeship in Baton Rouge." *Southern Review* 29 (Winter 1993): 58–66.

———. "From Romance to Ritual: Jean Stafford, Robert Lowell, and Catholicism." *Xavier Review* 12 (Spring 1992): 36–45.

Wolcott, James. "Blowing Smoke into the Zeitgeist: The Well-Deserved Resurrection of Jean Stafford." *Harper's*, June 1983, 57–59.

Bibliography

Avila, Wanda. *Jean Stafford: A Comprehensive Bibliography*. New York: Garland, 1983.

Index

The Author

Mary Ann Wilson, who received her Ph.D. from Louisiana State University, is assistant professor of English at the University of Southwestern Louisiana, where she formerly directed the freshman English program and currently teaches women's studies courses. She has taught at Louisiana State University and Georgia State University. Her articles on Jean Stafford and other women writers have appeared in the *Connecticut Review*, the *Xavier Review*, and the *Southern Review*.

The Editor

Gordon Weaver earned his B.A. in English at the University of Wisconsin-Milwaukee in 1961; his M.A. in English at the University of Illinois, where he studied as a Woodrow Wilson Fellow, in 1962; and his Ph.D. in English and creative writing at the University of Denver in 1970. He is author of several novels, including *Count a Lonely Cadence*, *Give Him a Stone*, *Circling Byzantium*, and most recently *The Eight Corners of the World* (1988). Many of his numerous short stories are collected in *The Entombed Man of Thule*, *Such Waltzing Was Not Easy*, *Getting Serious*, *Morality Play*, *A World Quite Round*, and *Men Who Would Be Good* (1991). Recognition of his fiction includes the St. Lawrence Award for Fiction (1973), two National Endowment for the Arts Fellowships (1974, 1989), and the O. Henry First Prize (1979). He edited *The American Short Story, 1945–1980: A Critical History*, and is currently editor of *Cimarron Review*. He is professor of English at Oklahoma State University. Married, and the father of three daughters, he lives in Stillwater, Oklahoma.